SUPPLY CHAINS UNSHACKLED

A Pragmatic Guide to Managing Global Supply Chains

Copyright © 2011 Sumantra Sengupta
All rights reserved.

ISBN: 1466379553
ISBN-13: 9781466379558

ABOUT THE BOOK

Supply Chains Unshackled is a book that has essentially been in the works for almost two decades. The core of the book is derived from several articles and best practice sections that I have authored in various supply chain related publications. The book deals with topics ranging from new planning paradigms to effective co-opetitive partnerships as well as multi-channel service chains.

The book is geared towards the busy executive who seeks to understand effective and seamless process; human factors and technology linkages that impact today's global supply chains as well as those who have been tasked with helping balance demand and supply in the ever changing and shifting consumer marketplace.

ABOUT THE AUTHOR

Sumantra Sengupta is an executive with two decades of experience in business, operations, and technology, with particular focus on Global Value Chain Management, Channel and Customer Service, and Business Resumption processes. He has led global business and technology strategy and implementation projects in the Retail, Consumer Products, Industrial Manufacturing, and Automotive industries in the US; APAC and EMEA geographies.

Currently, a Managing Director with EVM Partners LLC, he has previously served as a Vice President / Partner with several global and regional management consulting firms. He has also held Executive and Line positions with global CPG and enterprise software companies.

OTHER BOOKS BY THE AUTHOR

New Rules, Use information to unleash the hidden capital in the extended value community - published in 2002

Virtually Vertical, Pragmatic Guide to Streamlining the Corporation - published in 2010

This book is dedicated to my family for all their encouragement over the years and for believing in me even when the chips were down.

Thank You from the bottom of my heart.

TABLE OF CONTENTS

Introduction 8
Unshackled Part Zero – Teeing it Up 11
Unshackled Part I – Supply Chains or Extended
    Value Communities? 19
Unshackled Part II – New Measurement for Business
    Value Creation 35
Unshackled Part III– Top Ten Supply Chain Mistakes 51
Unshackled Part IV – Rethinking Supply Chain Planning. 67
Unshackled Part V– Planning for the Extended Supply Chains . . . 87
Unshackled Part VI – Multi Channel Management of
    Supply Chains. 105
Unshackled Part VII – B2B Exchanges – Non Traditional
    CoOpetition. 121
Unshackled Part VIII – Optimize Supply Chains and
    Avoid Data Explosion 135
Unshackled Part IX– Managing the Human Aspect of the
    Equation 147
Unshackled Part X – Strategic Information Management
    for the EVC 157
Unshackled Part XI - Technology and the Global Supply
    Chain. 173
Unshackled Part XII – Utilizing Mobility to enhance
    Supply Chains. 191
Unshackled Part XIII– Deciding Core and Non Core activities . . . 209
Unshackled Part XIV– Ten New Ideas for Value Creation . . . 221
Unshackled Part XV – Looking into the Crystal Ball. 237
Appendix. 243

AUTHORS NOTES

1. Unshackled Part III, IV, V, VI, VII, XII, and XIV are adapted from articles written by the author in various issues of Supply Chain Management Review. "This material is reprinted with permission of Supply Chain Management Review (www. scmr.com), copyright dates July/ August, 2004; Summer 1999; January/ February, 2008; November/ December, 2001; July/ August, 2000; September/ October 2011 and May/ June, 2009 respectively.

2. Unshackled Part VIII is adapted from an article that appeared in IIE Solutions and is Reprinted with permission from IIE Solutions Magazine, October 1996 with the permission of the Institute of Industrial Engineers, www.iienet.org, Copyright 2011"

INTRODUCTION

Do we really need another book on the value extraction needs within a supply chain? Aren't there many volumes dedicated to this topic? The answer to both these questions is a resounding" Yes". Well, then why add to the literature clutter? This book is different in the sense of scope and span of topics that are covered. It is a collection of articles and best practices that have been written and discussed over a period of 16 years by various companies that I have had the good fortune to consult with and work for. These constructs are not intended to be purely for discussion purposes since each and every chapter comprises of a set of constructs that have been implemented several times over. The client bases ranges from small start up's to large F500 companies in the US; Asia Pacific and Europe.

The book is intended to serve as a learning vehicle for busy executives who are charted with tackling varies issues that may evolve on a regular basis. The audience of this book are COO's; EVP and SVP of Supply Chains as well as Transformational CIO's who are seeking to gain a broad brush knowledge of what works and what does not work while implementing and optimizing their supply chains.

As with every book, there has to be some motivation for putting the time and effort required to bring this to print. After almost two decades in working with companies on their supply chain and related issues, I found that most of the constructs that I have championed have stood the test of time. I also found that I was referring clients to articles that were written by me in the mid to late 1990's. While searching the www. Channel can be quite effective; I decided to put many of my significant constructs under the "Unshackled" umbrella to make for a comprehensive read. .

The title *Supply Chains Unshackled* is very appropriate since every company that I have worked with seems to have a supply chain that is bound by some inherent inefficiency / constraints that serve as chains that bind progress and optimization. True value can only be generated by breaking the shackles that bind the company and serve as prevention against value creation. The constraints / shackles can be internally created or externally imposed. They range from insular executive thinking; poor process design and inadequate technology enablement. This book helps highlight ways to deal with many of the shackles that are faced by busy executives across the globe.

It is always hard to ensure that the right group of people receives the proper amount of heartfelt appreciation for their effort in bringing this book to market. I would also like to thank the many clients that I have had the privilege of serving and working with on various topics that are referenced in this book. There has been many a meeting in which one of these ideas was mercilessly beaten up and pressure tested. But the eventual outcome has always been one of mutual enhancement of the frameworks and hypotheses that have made their way into the final print.

I do not have enough words to thank my own family for the continued support that they have shown for me at all times. My wife, Veena, and our two boys, Sachin and Sanath, have always been my constant cheerleading section. The boys have probably made the biggest sacrifices in their current youth due to my travel schedule as well as the constant weekend workload required to complete this book. I can never compensate for the missed school plays and almost all other major functions, so I will not even try. Thank you Veena, Sachin, and Sanath.

Finally, I want to acknowledge the man who has been the guiding light of my life, my father, the Late Sanjoy Ranjan Sengupta, a man who was not only brilliant but also way ahead of his time. His physical guidance left me in 1991, but his metaphysical guidance persists even today

UNSHACKLED PART ZERO

Teeing It Up

I - THE FUNDAMENTALS

Supply Chains Unshackled is intended to serve as a practitioners' guide for topics in Supply Chain Management that range from hierarchical optimization to strategy formulation. The chapters are drawn from two decades of hardcore application and solutions provided to tough issues that have been faced in Manufacturing; Consumer and Retail Industry segments. The span of the book makes for good reading by the COO's; Heads of Supply Chains as well as CIO's who are tasked with enabling sound business strategies.

Supply Chains today can be summed up quite nicely by reading a recent book by Pietra Rivoli, *The Travels of a T-shirt in the Global Economy*, traced the global travels of a T-shirt that the author purchased on the sidewalks of Miami. It was quite revealing to see that the origin of the fabric for this simple product originated in Texas, but most subsequent processes were handled in countries where the labor arbitrage effect had the appropriate cost impact that allowed for a cost effective commercial launch. One just has to step back into his/her daily life to observe the huge impact that globalization and advances in technology are serving to make the world a lot flatter and more virtual for all of us. There was a time when we believed that proximity was a skill set for most of the activities that were an inherent part of our daily lives. However, that is now a thing of the past. Supply Chains have to keep us with this type of environment as well as deal with Financial institutions that have enabled on-line banking and bill payment, teller machines for asset transfers, voice response systems for generic questions, and when all else fails, a call to an operator working in Philippines or India. One has to wonder whether this lack of personalization for a strategic asset for all of us (i.e., cash) has the effect of further isolation of the human interactions that are woven into the fabric of a rapidly disappearing social society. The arguments of speed, control, and convenience are very legitimate, as is the balance of the benefits of a face-to-face human interaction. How many times have we made decisions on banks (mostly a commodity service) based on the fact that all things being equal, the customer service element swayed our decision and became the differentiators that won the business?

The fundamental economics of any corporation can be summarized by the equation Price = Cost + Margin or P = C + M. The days in which price was a derived variable determined by the margins that a company felt they could achieve are long gone. The consumable world today deals with prices that are fixed based on the end users tolerance and propensity to pay as opposed to being derived from a straight summation of total cost and desired margins. In this type of an environment, there are only two outcomes that are possible—rapid innovation and a razor sharp focus on all elements of total cost for a company to continue to create shareholder value.

Cost Management is not a new phenomenon. The field of Total Supply Chain management (TSCm) is now a board room topic in all major global corporations. TSCm primarily tackles the issues surrounding cost of goods sold (COGS), which accounts for approximately 50 to 70 percent of total costs in most corporations. The remainder of the costs is classified under sales, general and administrative (SG&A). However, as in most areas of focus, correct timing is a key factor in mass application and extensibility. TSCm did not begin to gain in popularity until the late 1980s when technological advances in decision support software began to emerge and the total cost of ownership of technology infrastructures began to follow Moore's Law and become affordable to corporations outside of the G100.

Almost every company that I deal with these days is attempting to gain a crisper understanding of their internal costs as well as process steps. Sometimes, I get a flashback to the days when most manufacturing companies dealt with the process of ABC cost analysis to segment the importance and value of every step. The detailed analysis of lifecycle economics for processes is now gaining in importance, just as the management of lifecycle economics for products gained in importance during the 1990s.

II - THE LAYOUT

Unshackled Part I: *Supply Chains or Extended Value Communities?*

Summary

Supply Chains have tended to be internally focused and inherently set up for sub optimization due to their span and scope. We believe that the new order of business optimization will force companies to inherently partner and team up with value added business partners both upstream and downstream in their business and operating model. We call that the Extended Value Community or EVC. This Part discusses the process of enabling an EVC that makes logical sense for your business and operating model.

Unshackled Part II: *New Measurement for Business Value Creation*

Summary

In this Part, we present a framework for quantifying and extracting business value that goes far beyond the traditional static measures of ROI (Return on Investment) and NPV (Net Present Value). Our measure called SVM (Sustained Value Measure) focuses on the organizations ability to extract and maintain the business value on a sustainable basis so that the bottom line of the company remains on the lower and better trajectory.

Unshackled Part III: *Top Ten Supply Chain Mistakes*

Summary

We often tend to repeat supply chain mistakes regardless of the industry segment we serve or dominate. The mistakes range from shortchanging the design aspect to attempting to be all things to all people by using the same supply chain. This Part is a concise description of the most common mistakes that companies make while designing their future state and provides tips on ways to avoid the mistakes.

Unshackled Part IV: *Rethinking Supply Chain Planning*

Summary

Supply Chain planning has been around for decades and yet we find that many companies still struggle with the traditional silos of production, materials management and distribution. Each department presents and provides constraints that inherently can be traded off against each other as long as they are handled simultaneously as opposed to sequentially. This Part presents a new framework to enable simultaneous optimization of the end to end supply chain.

Unshackled Part V: *Planning for the Extended Supply Chains*

Summary

As a follow up to the previous Part, supply chain planning for the extended enterprise or extended value communities is examined and constructs that work cross enterprise are examined. This Part combined with the previous one serves as a comprehensive way to plan your global, multi enterprise operations in a seamless fashion.

Unshackled Part VI: *Multi Channel Management of Supply Chains*

Summary

There are very few companies that are still single channel based for the delivery of their goods and services. This Part, examines constructs (operational and organizational) that enable companies to operate with the desired levels of agility across multiple channels while keeping in mind the inherent latencies and nuances of the channels.

Unshackled Part VII: *B2B Exchanges – Non Traditional Co Opetition*

Summary

Companies will always compete with each other based on their products and services. They will also compete on their inherent cost structures and associated advantages, However, one often finds that by pooling resources and functions that are inherently noncore or mutually advantageous, all participants win i.e. sum of the whole is much greater than the parts. This Part examines a construct that can guide effective sharing and winning in the marketplace.

Unshackled Part VIII: *Optimizing Supply Chains and Avoiding Data Explosions*

Summary

It is impossible to optimize the end to end supply chain (in the mathematical sense of the word). However, there are several pragmatic ways in which supply chains can be optimized locally while keeping in sight the global optimality. This Part provides a construct that can be utilized to drive optimal and timely decision making across the supply chain.

Unshackled Part IX: *Managing the Human Aspect of the Equation*

Summary

It is hard to create a baseline for the transformational journey, but there are certain industry characteristics that serve as helpful indicators. I present an analytical framework that allows a company to baseline its current state of virtualization as well as provides guidelines for areas to emphasize and augment to succeed in the effort.

Chapter Part X: *Strategic Information Management for the EVC*

Summary

Information Management capabilities are essential to the success of the any supply chain transformation within or external with an EVC. This Part provides IT leaders with a framework that is actionable and allows for clear distinction between a data centric approach to the EVC and an application centric approach. We also discuss various capabilities that are needed to effectively execute against the formation of a technology enabled supply chain.

Unshackled Part XI: *Information Technology and the Internal Supply Chain*

Summary

It is difficult to execute many key supply chain processes without the usage of information technology. This Part discusses various architectures and frameworks that can be used to optimize the usage of technology in the supply chain. The prior Part utilizes constructs that are applicable at the broader architecture level and this serves as a follow up for detailing the supply chain.

Unshackled Part XII: *Utilizing Mobility to enhance Supply Chains*

Summary

Mobility is quite ubiquitous these days and applications that utilize mobile data services are growing at a tremendous pace. However, behind all the hoopla it remains unclear what the true business benefits are of mass deployment and adoption of mobility. We present a framework and industry breakdown of potential applications and benefits for mobile usage.

Unshackled Part XIII: *Deciding Core and Non Core activities*

Summary

The debate continues about deciding what companies consider core and noncore processes and activities. While there is no right answer to this question, there are several points of view that can be effectively utilized to help executives gain alignment. This Part provides different methods of examining the problem from a pragmatic point of view.

Unshackled Part XIV: *Ten New Ideas for Value Creation*

Summary

We often tend to view supply chains as cost reduction centers and forget the value creation element that is equally lucrative. Value generation ideas range from being able to provide rapid innovation capabilities to the ability to deliver service oriented value add for products. This Part is a concise description of the most common value generating ideas to consider while designing the future state.

Unshackled Part XV: *Looking into the Crystal Ball*

Summary

The often asked question is "What next?" or "Now what?". While there are no crystal balls available to us, we do need to be able to provide some guidance based on the decades of experience. This final Part, highlights our best guesses on the future of supply chains and their associated impact on our business models.

Enjoy the rest of the book!

UNSHACKLED PART I

Supply Chains or Extended Value Communities?

In the global and flat world that we live and compete in today, it is common to see traditional industry competitors collaborate along the non-value-added processes so that the entire industry value chain can become more competitive so that it can withstand competitive entry from the upstart global companies. This leads us to the formulation of the construct of Extended Communities.

I. THE EXTENDED VALUE COMMUNITY OF AN ORGANIZATION

A holistic view of the extended value community

A community is defined as a group of people of like mind, or neighbors or members that share some kinship. If you apply the same concept to a company, you would arrive at an incorrect conclusion that a value community of an organization is a group of organizations that perform similar functions or businesses. However, the value community and its associated extension implies any group or function that is performing value-added activities for an organization beyond its traditional capabilities so that the end product or service is much more enhanced than without the value-added activity. The key words to focus on are *value added* and *enhanced*.

In our definition, value added is any activity that reduces the complexity of receiving the service or product for the end recipient. Complexity could be viewed as improved price effectivity, streamlined customer responsiveness, optimized information responsiveness, delightful end consumer interaction, and so on. Following similar logic, the word enhanced would apply to any activity that enhances the value-added variants in a positive manner not necessarily just faster or cheaper.

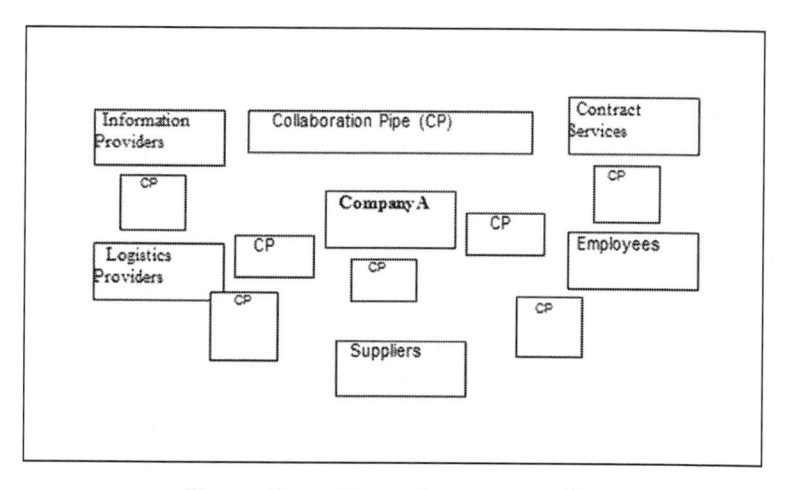

Figure One: The value community

The above figure demonstrates the concept of a value community for a generic company that makes use of necessary functions either by treating it as a competency or acquiring the services of other providers in order to fulfill their end commitment to deliver a quality product to a delighted consumer.

The elements of collaboration pipes that extend everywhere demonstrate that by exchanging information and products between partners, the entire value community of the company is enriched. Every provider exists in the value community of the company only because they are providing value-added services that make the end product better. If any provider falls shy of the two criterions or another provider can be found that can perform the same value add better, then the value community of the company should embrace the new entrant and reject the non-value-added entity.

Collaboration Pipes are an extremely important concept that glues together the participants in the virtually connected economy. These pipes serve as the information flow backbone as well as the cash flow mechanism for all the constituents in the value community. These are not technically engineered solutions but are a combination of the power of the resources involved in the exchange, the design surrounding the horizontal functions and the rules by which they are governed and finally the technology enablement that facilitates the real time or near real time sharing of information between the many to many relationships.

The consumer products industry has been using a variation of collaboration pipes to facilitate ECR (Efficient Consumer Response) and now CDNS (Consumer Driven Supply Network), which allows grocery retailers to communicate real time information back to the manufacturers to reduce overall inventory in the extended supply chain. The Extended Value Community (see Figure Two) enhances the concept of value community and extends it to be much more externally facing with customers, other competitors, as well as banks and finance institutions that make up the companies entire ecosystem. This involves construction of collaboration pipes with customers that allow for streamlining the supply chains as well as customer interactions. It also calls for collaboration in near real time with all aspects of financing and credit ratings that are extremely important not only for customers, but also for the manufacturers, retailers, as well as all other participants of the networked economy. The concept of collaboration pipes between traditional competitors is relatively new. While collaboration is good for the overall lowering of operating costs in the ecosystem and benefits the consumers, we should keep in mind the various competitive processes like new product development and branding strategies that will not lend themselves easily to competitive collaboration. We do propose that the concept of pooled spend to gain better leverage in volume discounts in non-core areas or areas that are not considered strategic will enhance the efficient use of working capital in many instances.

2. Traditional vs. Extended Community

The question that should be in our minds at this point is "What is the difference between the traditional and the extended communities?" The differences are subtle but many, and can be grouped by the major areas of focus, leverage, competitive nature, information management, closeness to customers, and participation in the networked economy.

Focus is defined as the default business philosophy that executives are comfortable in operating, that is, internal or within one's own company and associated partners who are directly involved in their supply chain, or external and with a view toward the betterment of the ecosystem of alliances and competitors.

Leverage is the defined as the amount of pooling and sharing of non-critical business information and assets that exists in the community. The varying degrees of leverage can range from purchasing leverage to complete outsourcing of parts of the value chain or delivery chain.

Competitive nature is defined by the extent to which a company can compete in today's consumer driven world by being internally focused or vertically integrated in their delivery pipe.

Area	Traditional	Value Community	Extended Value Community
Focus	Internal	Varies depending on function	External or Market facing
Leverage	Minimal	Some	Optimal
Competitive Nature	Not competitive	Competitive	Extremely Competitive but still focused on the brand
Information Management	Silos and disparate	Some sharing but mainly disparate	Common platform or data streams for strategic functions
Strength of Partnerships	Not strong	Strong based on functions	Strong in all functions and retains only core
Participation in Networked Economy	Minimal	Some	Key anchor for ecosystem

Figure Two: The Traditional to Extended spectrum

Information Management is an extremely important concept in the extended community. The traditional view that possession of information is power is mythical. All constituents demand that information should be accessible in near real time by all participants in the community, and the participant decides the analytic leverage that can be gauged from the use of the information. This goes against traditional wisdom that called for each participant second and third guessing the other in trying to satisfy ever-escalating consumer demands. A great example can be viewed in retail industry. As opposed to the retailer, manufacturer, and logistics providers all trying to predict end consumer demand, the use of collaboration pipes between the retailer and manufacturer and the logistics provider, with a view to using end sale or point of sale data, allows for working capital to be significantly reduced as well as allows fewer stock outs. However, we will acknowledge that this sharing of information in near real time can be quite difficult when various partners function on completely disparate systems and use non-homogeneous data streams and structures to perform analytical processes.

Strength of partnerships is always dependent and correlated to the concept of focus that a corporation maintains. The more internally focused its management, the more transactional the nature of the partnership. Strong partnerships are often found in environments in which there is an element of trust in the community and all members try to work for the common goal of a delighted and sustained revenue-generating customer. It also works well in industries in which no one company maintains a significant market ownership and is hence susceptible to the fickle consumer.

Participation in the networked economy or the connected economy is often a culmination of the behaviors that are listed above that area. Companies that participate in the connected economy often tend to be focused on building and differentiating their superior brand and market position and striping themselves of many non-core activities in a shared service or outsourced virtual model.

Leverage, as we have discussed before, is extremely key for success in the new economy. In traditional thinking, the amount of leverage of core competencies is minimal as companies try to do everything themselves from manufacturing to distribution, sales, and marketing. This ends up diluting the initial starting purpose of any corporation. Leverage and focus often are interchangeable. This is due to the simple fact that the more focus shift that occurs in a company from internal to being value community based and finally to the extended value community, the better is the leverage of core competencies that we will find in the organization. Not everyone can be good at everything, hence the need to find the two or three key processes in which to excel becomes greatly needed as EVCs begin to compete with other EVCs as opposed to companies competing in the new economy. This implies that the leverage of outside capabilities increases as one moves across the focus spectrum in an inversely proportional fashion. A prime example of leverage and focus on competencies is Dell Computer. The simple model of a build or configure to order has as well as going direct to consumer allowed the company to achieve significant operational leverage over its nearest competitors. This also includes the application of various sorts of outsourcing and ventures that allow the company to focus on its core competencies of marketing, customer service, and product development.

Some characteristics that lend themselves extremely well to the move are strong brand driven products, products that are mainly commodities, presence of a large number of contract service providers, passing information between participants relatively simple due to the degree of trust, presence of key number of strategic suppliers driven by the common good of the entire ecosystem, and so on.

he third criterion of competitiveness is probably debatable by the classical theorists needs careful analysis. Classical thinking always has argued that the more vertically integrated the company, the better positioned it is in order to compete. This thinking is inherently based on the assumption that every company has the time in the market and the resources needed to eventually gain excellence in all aspects of business. The fallacy lies in the fact that consumers and customers are unwilling to provide protracted periods of trial and error processes to even the leading edge companies in the world. That coupled with the fickle mind of consumers, shortening product life cycles, and globalization, inherently allows no room for error in all aspects of business. This need in the marketplace has facilitated the rise of companies that focus and build core competencies that are horizontal in nature, that is, distribution, sales, and marketing, and so on, that can be leveraged across multiple companies and allow the participating companies to become more competitive by improving the top and bottom lines. This leads us to the fact that as companies continue to focus on competencies as well as leverage their resources in a networked manner, they become more competitive in participation in the networked economy.

3. The Economic Power of the Value and the Extended Community

There are no cookie cutter formulae that can easily quantify either impact, but we will discuss a concept called Sustained Value Measure (SVM) that provides a framework for evaluating returns from value and extended value communities. Using empirical analysis and measures, we have seen returns that follow an interesting phenomenon of "Equality >> Partiality."[5] The concept has demonstrated that the economic sum of the parts is almost always inferior to the whole by factors that are in excess of 30 to 40 percent of the total cost figures.

So where is the economic power base in these communities? The answer is "everywhere and nowhere." The power is inherent in the community and not concentrated in any one constituent. The parts have to work together to benefit themselves and the whole. If any part attempts to tilt the balance unfavorably for its personal benefit, the entire community can reject the part and infuse a new one. The rejected constituent is now relegated to either its former self or has to create a new extended value community. The barriers to creation are many and complex, and cause immediate loss of competitive benefits that will never be recouped.

4. Key Steps for Migration to the Extended Value Community

There are no known shortcuts, prepackaged time phased solutions, or associated benefit streams that work across all industries. The key tenants that dictate the timeframe as well as rapid realization of the freed up capital are based on four key factors. They are as follows: segmentation of process areas; ability to attract and retain value community anchors; readiness of the extended community to disrupt status quo; and finally the ability to execute the vision. A potential phasing is illustrated in Figure Four.

<u>Segmentation of process areas:</u> The key task for the formation of any EVC is the ability to dissect core and non-core process areas that are candidates for deploying collaboration pipes. This deployment is heavily dependent on the associated leverage that is added to the top line or subtracted from the bottom line. Sample process areas for analysis can be adapted from the various frameworks presented in Chapter One, which included all front office functions like customer service, order management, and fulfillment, as well as back office functions like payroll processing, production and material control, information technology, and research and development. These process areas all have associated strategic leverage as well as cost/value equations or propositions. The segmentation process should be focused on at least three dimensions. The dimensions are strategic vs. non-strategic for the business, customer value add vs. minimum necessity to perform baseline customer service, and core competency vs. non-core. An example of strategic, non-core, customer value add is customer service call centers that respond to inquiries as well as perform returns processing. Another example of non-strategic, non-core, and minimum necessity is the process of procuring MORO (maintenance repair and operations) items. The first example dictates that a dedicated and closely monitored collaboration pipe be constructed and that the community infrastructure needs to bear the associated expense while the close monitoring and complete dedication of a collaboration pipe is questionable for the second. The second process allows the EVC to gain high economic impact while minimizing direct expenditures on information technology. Using similar logic, the community can construct a value roadmap for the horizontal processes and the associated value propositions that include the various types of collaboration pipes that are needed between participants. This roadmap also allows the community to take a closer look at their strategic leverage points that may exist

in the participants (independent operations), but are eroded when the community is created due to long-term contracts and lack of effective substitutes.

Ability to Attract Value Community Anchors: This process marks a crucial turning point from the theoretical concept of the value community to realizing the industry readiness and acceptance of the concept. The anchors are defined as the first set of companies to create shared leverage and collaboration pipes. This is also the point in which the originator of the idea or the key anchor demonstrates their willingness to share equitably in the joint wealth creation or working capital efficiency model. Many a great idea has withered at this point due to excessive need of the key anchor to control the economic outcomes. The value community should be created such that all participants are treated as equals with a degree of fair share allocation of top line growth and bottom line savings. If the community is managed or hosted by a neutral third party for other value-added services, then the allocation needs to be net of management fees.

Readiness of an anchor is extremely key for the phasing in of project delivery. It needs to be evaluated along four dimensions: technology readiness, business readiness, executive readiness, and market readiness.

Business Readiness: Any company that desires to leverage others' skill sets end expertise in a functional area, should enable their internal processes and metrics of their own people to be conducive to a healthy partnering environment as opposed to one in which partnering is viewed as an internal failure. The processes should be as modular as possible in order to effectively decouple the portions that are better suited for outside assistance. Also, the internal metrics of the resources that will be needed to enable the smooth transition to the partner needs to be structured to enable a positive and professional work environment that is conducive to extremely productive work.

Executive Readiness: The whole concept of migration from a vertically integrated model to a semi virtual or completely virtual model is as much a function of an exercise to determine core competency, as it has to do with an executive's psychological frame of mind and state of mind while enabling a decision. A colleague of mine from Europe once drew an executive's psychological profile during the course of an extremely strategic outsourcing decision. It resembled a dual bell shaped curve with the first peak that was extremely steep and petered off extremely quickly. The peak dealt with the positive enthusiasm that the executive brought to the decision making and the rapid petering was a result of peer pressure that the executive faced from others who were not as forward thinking as he was. The second peak was one in which the executive was not only enthusiastic about the decision but was armed to the teeth with every fact to back up the strategic decision. The deal was signed after the second peak and the petering of that peak was nothing but a matter of tying up some loose ends on the financials and other factors. It is extremely important for all parties (executive, partners, consultants, etc.) to maintain a fact-based decision-making mindset throughout the entire process that will allow for a less emotional process and a much more productive outcome.

Market Readiness: This extremely crucial readiness factor needs some discussion. Industries tend to mature at their own pace and time. Sometimes major shifts and movements occur in the basic structure of an industry (like the advent of digitization in the publishing world or the advent of electronic bill payment to the postal community) that facilitates the rapid transition of industrial models. In cases where the fundamental business model and associated value proposition is extremely well entrenched and is not threatened by the advent of either new technology or new competitors, it is relatively hard to create new models and shift the paradigm that persists in that industry structure. The automotive industry is a great example of such an industry where improvements have been relatively along the lines of similar business models as opposed to fundamentally shifting ones. While change has occurred, the structure of the industry and the associated network has not been altered much. The high-technology industry on the other hand has seen rapid changes as well as fundamentally different business models due to the existence of constantly emerging new entrants as well as cheaper substitutes.

Technology Readiness: The ability of a company to participate in any form of an EVC is heavily dependent on the current state of affairs as it relates to data accessibility, integrity, and ability to share strategic information with other value-added members of the EVC. We have often found that the companies that are the most willing to share data and information are also the most incapable of providing data that is accurate and timely in order to make any meaningful impact on a business. A small study for a category that was performed with some key retailers in the U.S. showed that many of them were extremely willing to participate in any EVC that would bring a significant impact to their top and bottom line financial performances, but less than 25 percent were capable of providing meaningful and accurate data in a timely fashion. This demonstrated that the way to construct the EVCs for some of these companies would have to entail a significant amount of time and technology investment that needed to be factored into any implementation plan.

We have found that the rapid formation and acceptance of EVCs is more likely to occur in industries that have a need to constantly reinvent themselves for fear of losing significant market share, as well as in industries where there is a significant amount of wasted capital across the various categories of fixed and working. While first mover advantage is extremely crucial, it is also important to move at the right time so that the new model within the context of an EVC retains a high probability of gaining success in the industry.

While choosing anchors, some other key criterion are preexisting trustworthy business relationships, being viewed as long-term strategic partners and /or competitors, similarity in operations so that processes and collaboration pipes can be standardized to a certain degree, and stability of market share amongst participants, that is, no anchor should be on their last leg as a corporation with consistently declining market share.

The last point is important to understand as we find that marriages of equals or near equals in terms of market share as well as complementary products or capabilities will be the EVCs that will be able to withstand the various pressures that come along with collaboration and coordination.

Readiness of EVC to change status quo: While the steps for the creation of a value community are easily replicated for the EVC, it is extremely important to point out a couple of key differences between the two. These are the ability and willingness of customers to share collaboration pipes and the desire of all participants to disrupt the status quo in the industry niche to enable sustained revenue growth.

We have found that in many customers (a key ingredient in the creation of EVC), the ability and the willingness for efficient use of collaboration pipes are not convergent, that is, the willing customers are not able to handle the complexity of a collaboration pipe (near real time) due to lack of process discipline and relevant technology enablement. And those that have the capacity have little intention of opening up collaboration pipelines into the community as it is often perceived naively as a loss of control. Unfortunately, there is no easy solution to the problem, and the resolution of the issue in terms of customer acceptance plays a huge factor in the economic viability of the EVC.

The desire to disrupt the status quo in an industry niche is driven by the need to reduce complexity in any EVC, that is, the number of stages and the number of links or handoffs that occur prior to reaching the end consumer or customer. We have found that every industry globally can afford to reduce the complexity and not sacrifice customer service in any significant manner. The reduction effort is facilitated by the efficient use of collaboration pipes to eliminate both physical and virtual entities by replacing assets, inventory, and time lags in the community with near real time information.

Ability to Execute: This final stage makes or breaks great ideas and value propositions. The execution of the idea implies different things to varying audiences. For the finance folks in an EVC, it means securing the appropriate type of debt or equity finance as well as the appropriate credit lines that allow for a reasonable WACC (weighted average cost of capital) as well as constant monitoring of the proposed sources of revenue. The supply chain functions need to execute aggressively on the agreed to horizontal functions like logistics, purchasing, and so on, while the sales and marketing functions need to violently execute the sales and marketing plan that will enable the EVC to be successful in a sustained manner.

4. Setting the Framework for Emerging Process Areas in SCM, CCM, SM, and B2anyone

Supply Chain Management (SCM) in an EVC is centered on concepts of collaboration, coordination, and uniform visibility across all participants. Excellence in the traditional silos of planning, manufacturing, logistics, and purchasing is relevant but less strategic for each individual silo and extremely important and strategic for the coordinated EVC.

The key issues facing SCM in an EVC are: (1) collaborative response to any demand signal, (2) connected commerce that resets commerce points based on shifting yields, and (3) collaborative and coordinated buying based on shifting dynamic variables.

We will discuss each of these in greater detail later in the book. The key element that requires highlighting is the emergence of supply chain activities as a strategic and competitive lever as opposed to a back office function. The evolution of EVCs will allow SCM to become the key differentiator that will allow the various communities to compete and help in sustained wealth creation for all participants.

Customer Centric Management (CCM) in an EVC is all about providing personalized service to all constituents across all horizontal functions that are deployed in the EVC. This implies that there is an evolving need for CCM and SCM professionals to work side by side, as opposed to silos, as the points of origination for user requests shift across the links and need response from both groups.

The key issues facing CCM in an EVC are (1) dynamic resetting of user expectations across all participants, (2) dynamic management of channel conflicts across all horizontal functions and users, and (3) blurring of service and supply chain management functions in the eyes of the end consumers.

As EVCs become more prominent and end user expectations skyrocket, the one that will delight the majority of their participants will win the war of the "sticky" consumer.

Supplier Management (SM) in an EVC needs careful mapping. We often discover that suppliers in one EVC are consumers in another and, hence, will require having an essence of "split personalities," and will need to respond to requirements that are of differing and often conflicting sorts. This is one area that little time and effort has been utilized expended till date in most EVCs.

The key issues facing SM in an EVC are (1) collaborative and dynamic reaction to shifting user requirements, (2) brand dilution due to extensive participation in multiple EVCs and (3) need to standardize information, data, and processes across multiple EVCs.

B2anyone (B2a) is the fundamental platform on which any EVC is constructed. A lot has been done in the area of B2C and B2B, but the new rules require business be conducted between any and all participants. This will need construction of evolving commerce rules, financing rules, and physical and information infrastructure needs. The shift of economic power from single enterprise to distributed enterprises adds to the complication.

The key issues facing B2a are (1) the need to change the status quo and disrupt industry structures to enable sustained wealth creation, (2) evolution of business frameworks as well as information management constructs to support distributed power, and (3) the need to shift from large horizontal areas of focus to be narrower in focus and specific to industries.

So, the fundamental issue that we must wrestle with before a transformational launch is to engage in an industry specific scan and decide whether to sole anchor the partnered process or offer to engage equal or smaller partners in the creation of shared services or common processes that would enable the elimination of waste and process redundancies from the entire industry's value chain. These extensions can be offered to core suppliers as well as channel partners (distributors) who derive a large percentage of their own business revenue by being a captive partner of the larger entity. There are several examples of such industry specific collaboration along non-value-added processes, like physical transportation, information technology infrastructure, back office finance, and human resource functions, as well as generic customer touch points like call centers.

The future of EVCs is closely aligned to the adoption success of B2a concepts, but does not tie to the success of any particular B2 initiative. This implies that while some concepts may face a challenge in gaining economic success in the connected world, overall sustained economic growth lies in sound business fundamentals.

So, are we ready for the onslaught of EVCs? Only the test of time will dictate whether macro industries will prevail over micro companies. All indicators imply an increased focus on the end consumer and rapid improvements to the top and bottom line. This, coupled with the focus on core competencies, bodes extremely well for the formation of EVCs. Recent advances in information technology make the deployment possible and enable the concept to fully materialize in the near future.

NOTES FROM CHAPTER

UNSHACKLED PART II

New Measurement for Business Value Creation

1. Defining Sustained Value Measure (SVM)

The key for success in the new economy is for companies and the associated EVCs to deliver sustained value to all its participants and channel partners as well as value-added service providers. The emphasis on sustained value is key to the overall success of the new economy. Too often, we have observed companies providing rapid returns on investment and being rewarded in the short term by the financial markets. However, in the long run, only those companies that provide well-defined value propositions for the institutional investors are rewarded with large market capitalization. I can recall a discussion with the global head of supply chain for one of the leading consumer products companies on the topic of inventory management and its associated impact on shareholder value. An extremely keen observation that came out of that discussion was that only those companies (like Dell and Cisco) that have fundamentally made shifts to their underlying business model and, hence, associated working capital leverage, have been rewarded by the financial markets in the long run. Other companies that have made incremental improvements to their inventory turns by using information more intelligently have not been rewarded handsomely in the long run by the financial community.

So, given that value communities have existed in varying forms over the years and information management has been used effectively in the partial communities in varying degrees, why do we feel the need to define a different value measure for the new economy and the EVC concept? Why should the standard success measures for information management projects like return on investment (ROI), return on invested capital (ROIC), internal rate of return (IRR), or net present value (NPV) not hold true in the new economy? We are not claiming that these measures are flawed, but the content and the major areas of improvement that contributes to these measures require new thinking. Two factors that affect the computation of the measures adversely are listed below in no particular order:

- Assumes linear processes
- Not focused on degree of sustainability

Assumes linear processes: This has been an area of constant debate in recent years. We have seen the advent of virtual models in many industries as well as the appearance of dynamic markets that serve many anchors within and across industries. However, the improvement areas that are targeted, like demand pipeline management, customer intimacy, service level improvements, and so on, tend to assume that the processes are the traditional linear processes as opposed to the dynamic and circular processes in the impacted areas like those in an EVC. This tends to make the calculations that are factored into the ratios focus on the incremental improvements as opposed to the focus of total market satisfaction of all members and the interdependencies that are inherent in the new economy. An example of this is the service level improvements that are often shown as benefit streams in any customer management project as well as most demand pipeline improvement initiative. These ratios are calculated in functional silos and it is assumed that the processes are sequential and linear as opposed to interrelated and circular. This leads to incorrect classification and some double counting of the associated benefit streams.

Not focused on degree of sustainability: I am sure that all of us have faced situations in which the benefit streams that were promised were never realized due to the inability of the organization to change or process the turmoil that large swings in business models bring to the community. This is an area of concern for us in the implementation of any EVC as it is the people who have to change their behavior that is often learned over many years. We feel that in order for any improvement to be sustained, the key process changes have to be championed and made part of the day-to-day business management of the EVC in order for all members to experience the sustained revenue stream that goes with the process.

While these are just some issues that we have faced in our travels in many industries and initiatives, it is by no means an exhaustive list or an implication that all initiatives have fallen prey to the problems. We recognize that there are many ways to solve these issues, and present a sample framework based on the concept of Sustained Value Measure and attempt to resolve most of the issues that we have commented on previously.

The framework is fairly simple when viewed in light of the observations that were made in the prior section. There are four anchors around which it is built. These anchors are kept in synch with each other via the interdependency loops. All these four anchors and the loop interaction together add up to provide the SVM for any EVC and its use of information to drive sustained value. The measure is a cash flow analysis over the time frame that we are expecting the EVC to operate within and provide benefit to its members.

Anchors

The four anchors (see Figure Four) are: Source driven Improvement, New Models, Collaboration Value, and Repetitive Measure. Each of these elements has a strong information management influence that facilitates the varying benefit streams that can be garnered for the participating companies. It is important to note that we are not claiming that every benefit stream needs to be based on the better leverage of information or the implementation of any technology elements. We have found that in excess of 70 percent of the work in the new economy is steeped in either better use of existing information or augmentation of current information sources to gain competitive advantage.

Source Driven Improvement: This aspect of SVM is probably the best-understood element. It deals with free cash flow improvements that can be made by optimizing the C.O.L.E. factors in the internal process areas from the frameworks.

New Models: The new economy implies constant re-evaluation of the business and market facing strategies for participating companies. This is largely due to the fact that intense competition and globalization requires a higher degree of adaptive behavior from its participants. The days of static information and business structures that provide competitive advantage for companies is long gone. Imitation is often considered the best form of flattery but has also given rise to low-cost providers that compete for the same shelf and eye space of the end consumer. While consumers have become more demanding in the recent years, they have also become somewhat less discerning regarding the brand message that used to allow for constant differentiation. This does not imply that brand differentiation is dead but is an indicator that companies with branded products need to be in a constant mode of new product and capability introduction that will allow the gap between them and the nearest imitator to continue to expand.

New models that have a strong impact on the type of information intelligence that EVCs need to focus on are in two areas: adaptability and invention. The future of EVCs is in being able to adapt to the changing and shifting needs of the customer base. Adaptive behavior is a combination of the people, end consumers, investments, and the industry that is being served by the EVC. In order to capture the people element of the new model and its associated benefit stream, it is important to gauge and evaluate the speed in which the organization can adapt, as well as the number of internal ideas that are generated by the members of the participating companies. In today's global world, it is also important that the ideas scale meets the expanding needs of the constituent markets. A great example of a company that cherishes its internal idea generation is 3M Corporation. The story of Post-It notes and how they came into existence is well documented. That is the type of innovative thinking from within the ranks that will set apart EVCs. It is important to allow people access to all relevant information that can lead to new product designs based on evolving customer needs. This implies that information accessibility is a key factor for all people within any EVC. This coupled with the encouragement from management to participate in "out-of-the-box" thinking is a key element that requires quantification. The same logic can be applied to end consumer adaptability in an EVC. This deals with the ability of the EVC to provide the customers with an array of choices and provide degrees of customization that makes them feel empowered.

The area of invention is extremely important to enable investors and potential investors to gauge the long-term viability of the business model as well as the industry. Invention is the key element that allows for new products and improvements to products, as well as new services related to products, to keep the revenue model enhanced and refreshed from an end consumer perspective. Too often, we have seen companies that have an abundance of cash cows but very few inventions in the pipeline. These EVCs and participating companies are headed for a disastrous result in the financial market once the demand for the current product is saturated. In addition to the new product pipeline, it is also important to quantify the invention fostering culture that is prevalent in the EVC. It is the culture that will allow for the members and participants to reward employees for innovative thinking as well as the extra mile that is often required in order to bring new inventions to market. The fostering culture is a combination of management support, the introduction process, as well as the technical competence that employees and members possess. This coupled with the ability of management to set aside significant funds to fuel future growth is an essential component of the new model.

Collaboration Value: A key element in EVCs is the ability to collaborate and share information within and across industries. The sharing of information between traditional competitors as well as other value-added service providers enables the EVC to take a holistic view toward streamlining the demand pipelines that exist in the industry as opposed to silos of excellence. Collaboration is often misrepresented in the popular press as the ability to work in an environment that fosters the exchange of information and results, thereby allowing participants to reach a consensus driven outcome. This definition of collaboration is only partially correct. In the EVC world, collaboration is akin to the complete outsourcing of key functions in the supply chain to a third party or one of the anchor members, who will focus on the function completely and develop world class competencies in the area. This implies that other members will rely on the service provider for the fulfillment of that function. Collaboration is always across all channels as well as major process areas. We predict that the future of EVCs will allow for the development of centers of competency within each community. We will find that purchasing, logistics, manufacturing, and information technology management will be some of the key areas for collaboration. We also maintain that areas such as research and development and quality will be collaborative in the traditional sense of the word as opposed to dynamic EVC related. This will immediately drive improvements to the top and bottom line in any EVC, as world class capabilities will imply that the achievement of Class A programs in all areas will be a reality as opposed to a pipe dream. This, coupled with the capabilities in the EVCs to be technologically enabled to share information in near real time and in a standardized format, will create the optimal structured industry from an end consumer perspective. It is important to note that this area of collaboration is a fertile ground for double counting the benefits gained from operations improvement. We will discuss the key factors that will enable us to isolate the benefit derived from this alone in the next section.

Repetitive Measure: This is the key measure that ensures that the promised land of EVC benefit is delivered to all participants. This is the area for violent execution of strategies, ideas, and concepts. Repetitive measure ensures that process changes are executed and adhered to, as well as appropriate metrics adapted, to help modify human behavior so that the value streams are realized in perpetuity or as long as the duration of the stream will allow. It is key to note that many great ideas remain undervalued and undercapitalized due to the financial community's lack of belief in the execution ability of the constituent. Repetitive measure can be quantified by focusing on the ability for technology enabled EVC to execute on three components. They are managerial, operational, and external aspects of the vision or plan.

Managerial aspect of execution includes the ability of upper management to focus on key business issues and strategic guidelines, align compensation policies to gain organizational motivation toward the same goals, and maintain laser sharp focus on the quality of motivation and drive of the key team members as well as the quality of the renewed vision. These aspects are hard to quantify but are extremely important if the entire corporation is to succeed in breaking new ground.

Operational aspect of execution is closely tied in to the operational benefit stream that was discussed earlier with the caveat that the executional view must maintain a constant vigil on the end consumer and value-added service provider satisfaction. While the consumer satisfaction is well understood and the ramifications of not performing are also well documented in the annals of business, we are not certain that the view to maintain satisfaction of key service providers has been well understood. In today's virtual world, it is extremely important to treat contract resources as an extension of the immediate internal silo. This will facilitate the same type of cultural tie in with the parent community and will allow for the entire EVC to be aligned along similar lines. A colleague of mine from a strategy consulting firm explained this concept extremely concisely by stating that we should look at service providers with an eye to understand whether we would trust them with our own wallets. If the answer is affirmative, then we have a strategic alliance, else we have a doomed relationship.

The external aspect of execution attempts to quantify the corporate culture of the EVC. Corporate culture can often be viewed as the competitive differentiator in the final stages of a business development cycle. Everyone would like to work with a company that mirrors and complements its own key belief system. While this is again fairly hard to quantify, it is important to look at areas like brand image, employee satisfaction and productivity, and the ability of the EVC to attract and retain valuable resources.

Interdependency Loop: By now, two issues should be clear to the reader. The first is the danger of double and triple counting the benefit streams that arise from each area when viewed as a silo, and the second deals with the contribution of information management in the overall value equation of the EVC. The application if the interdependency loop deals with the two issues. The main job of the loop is to maintain a programmatic view of the benefit streams and the associated interdependencies between the four anchors and to apply a percentage benefit that is derived for the EVC by the better use of information management as opposed to an area that can be executed in complete vacuum from the technology layer. This loop plays the policing role for the EVC to help determine the key areas for investment in new and emerging technologies as opposed to areas that require little or no investments.

2. Calculating SVM

The analytics behind SVM are fairly straightforward once the areas of benefit have been identified and the percentage contribution of the information aspect has been applied by the loop. The key to successful computation of these areas lies in the segmentation of all proposed revenue streams based on the segmentation of the anchors. This is probably the most time consuming part of the entire exercise and requires complete executive buy-in and support to gain and reach consensus. Figure 1, shows a framework that has been used in a couple of instances for EVC creation, and seems to work well.

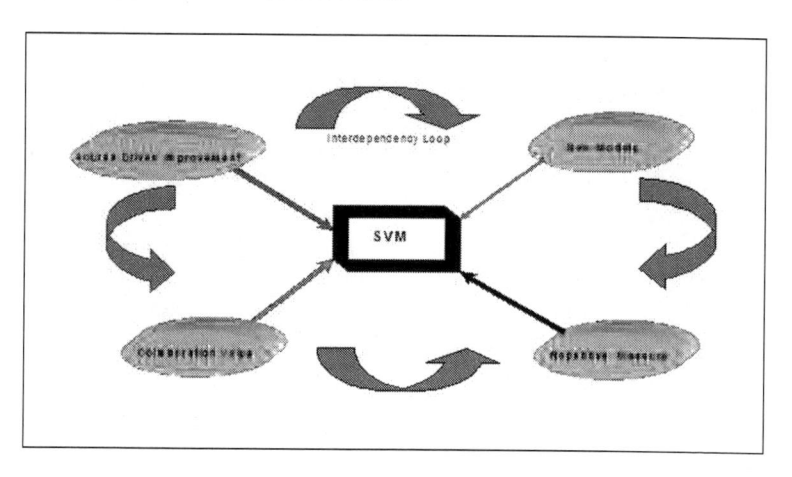

Figure 1: An SVM Framework

We show the areas of benefit under a common theme of e/m/t. This outlines the evolving channels that exist for commerce related activities in any EVC. "E" is for electronic, "m" is for the wireless enabled channel, and "t" demonstrates the traditional bricks and mortar channel. The benefit streams are divided into four areas: collaboration for customer satisfaction, virtual partner opportunity, link opportunity, and optimized commerce opportunity. Collaboration is stated in detail in section one. Virtual partner opportunity demonstrates the value levers gained from strategic partnerships and alliances. Link demonstrates the value derived from better connectivity and sharing of key information between trading partners. This is closely tied to the discussion on new models in section one. The optimized commerce area deals with new models as well as operational efficiency that were discussed in section one. We show some of the major categories for impact quantification in Figure 2 below. The legend is H – High Impact, M – Medium Impact, and L – Low Impact.

Working Capital	Inventory turns	H	H	H	M
Fixed Capital	Asset leverage	L	H	H	M
Service Level	As measured by key customers	H	H	H	M
Strength of partnerships	Degree of virtuality and dis-intermediation	L	H	H	M
Market Penetration	Number of new channels, geographies and product innovation	L	M	L	H
Revenue Lift	In stock percentage at end consumption point	L	M	H	H
Ecosystem Alignment	Metrics of participants that are in common	L	L	M	H

Figure 2: Sample computational metrics

While the analytics behind the computation of the metrics will differ from instance to instance, it is extremely important to note that all participating member computations need to be a part of the overall benefit of the EVC. Often the fallacy that we have seen being made to computations is the assumption of static measures and static models that lead to incremental improvements. It is key to evaluate the changing business models that allow the EVC to decrease working capital by factors of 100 percent and the fixed capital that exists on the books of the company by similar factors. These will happen by changing the business models of companies as opposed to modifying the current business models. The infiltration of various channels for commerce, for example, web, physical, and mobile, need to be factored into the computation of the revenue lifts and working capital efficiencies. We need to factor in the new product pipeline as well as the degree of innovation of current pipeline that exists for the various participants. The best method of computing the revenue related to innovation and new products is to study the potential size and penetration in the market as well as the degree of cannibalization that will occur to existing product lines.

While the above figure is fairly self-explanatory, we should not dwell on the relative ranks that have been assigned, as they will be extremely case dependent. The working capital measure of inventory as well as payables and receivables have been known to increase significantly by collaborating with the partners on various demand and supply changes as well as being able to outsource portions of non-value-added activities for the core set of anchors. This facilitates that partnerships be viewed as strategic and alliances and be viewed as extensions of the core anchor set. While we have not found that dynamic commerce is a huge contributor to the inventory turns, it is also a matter of time before the whole "bid-ask" or auction process is extended to a larger group of products and channels to enable much more open participation by multiple suppliers and partners globally in order to continue to extend and improve the EVC.

Fixed capital leverage is often achieved when portions of a process is either outsourced or rationalized. It is impacted greatly by being able to receive real time information from partners regarding patterns of service and sales that exist in the field in order to facilitate the closure or offloading of assets that provides minimal lift to customer service.

Service levels are often viewed as a direct correlation to the working capital metric, but the difference that we would like to emphasize is that it should be measured through the customer's eyes and not the internal constituents. We have often found that internal measures are extremely inflated due to inherent bad practices in order management and sales that cause missed orders and shipments to be treated in a much different manner than the customer's measure.

Market penetration is a well-understood measure that can be used for existing product lines as well as emerging product lines. The key trend that we have observed is that the use of the emerging channels of technology can quite significantly boost the accessibility to customers in various geographies that were either not served or under served in the past. This is one area in which the commerce influence is quite high while the others are somewhat less.

Revenue lift closely tracks market penetration but has an added twist that allows in-stock levels to significantly increase by sharing demand flow through information as well as dynamic pricing data between the various partners. This is often the basis for collaboration between partners in the new economy and allows entire industries to become more competitive.

Finally, the ecosystem alignment measure completes the dollarized value of the EVC. It is key to use this as a measure of productivity of the EVC as aligned metrics will lead to a more functional group of individuals who work to a common end goal as opposed to conflicting objectives.

The final step in the quantification is to apply an ID Factor to the entire value. An ID Factor is the Interdependency Loop factor (a number less than 100 percent) that is a measure of the potential double counting that may occur due to interdependencies in the various computations. It can also be used as a measure of the amount of key interdependency that may result in not achieving the overall value. An IDF of 80 percent shows that there is 20 percent potential of overlap in the value streams but is hard to isolate due to the intricate dependencies. It can also be read as the fact that the tasks are so inter-related that there is an 80 percent probability that the value stream will be realized. This is the SVM that can be translated into shareholder value or potential upside to shareholder EPS (see Figure 3).

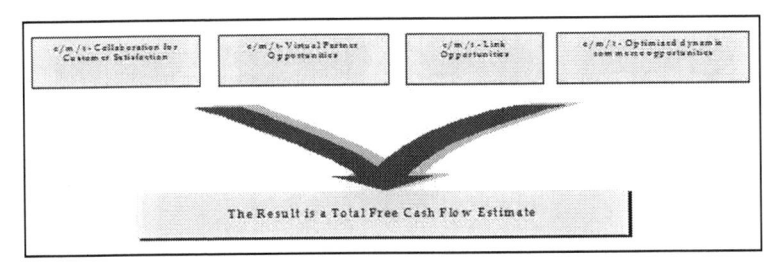

Figure 3: Sample SVM calculation

While the above method gives the entire SVM for the EVC, it requires another couple of steps to generate the SVM for information management within the EVC. The first step is to distinguish the factor (0<factor<1) by which information management impacts a related measure directly as opposed to a measure that is more driven by process discipline and the people. This factor is applied to the SVM to generate the portion of SVM that is non-information management related. The second step requires a factor (0<factor<1) to be multiplied to the resulting number from step one that will provide the degree of repetitive application of the information management that is needed to generate a sustained value to the community. This resulting dollarized number is the SVM due to information management and the remainder of the dollar from the first step is the one-time impact of information management. This is the SVM that can be translated into shareholder value or potential upside to shareholder EPS.(see Figure 4 below)

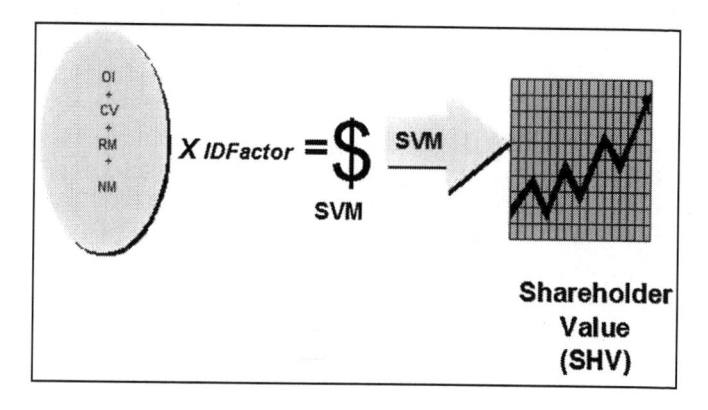

Figure 4: Convert EVC Impact to Shareholder Value

3. Why is it appropriate for all coopetetive companies?

Does SVM imply that the old measure of ROI is dead? That is by no means our intention or the message that we have attempted to deliver. We feel that ROI is still an extremely valid measure, but the contributing factors that are used to derive the calculation are outdated and do not mirror the reality of the new economy. The major changes that have occurred are the breakdown of the vertically integrated company, the rapid use of technology to provide seamless information flow between all constituents, globalization impacts of new markets and channels, and the advent of "co-opetition" amongst traditional competitors to provide value to all constituents by the pooling and leveraging of combined volumes and areas of competency.

The old adage that companies do not compete but supply chains do is soon going to give way to the fact that supply chains do not compete but value communities do. This will be a key shift in the way that the old economy companies are valued in the eyes of the financial community. This implies that the future for both the new economy and old economy companies lies in the leverage of the core competencies and the creation of virtual competencies for the non-core ones. The future also demands that co-opetition needs to happen rapidly to counter the static and sometimes declining growth in various categories. Finally, in a service-oriented economy where products are getting commoditized and services are gaining ground, the people and the innovation that exists within the community will be heavily rewarded as the future source of sustained revenue. All this and more are captured in the essence of SVM and hence its applicability for the future of the new economy.

Summary

This chapter provided a perspective around process extensibility as well as valuation mechanisms for non-value-added processes that can be applied in a co-opetitive industry setting. However, this requires the possession of a collaborative and industry improvement mindset as opposed to the normally prevalent "what's in it for me and me alone" frame of reference. This has to be coupled with market readiness and acceptance for co-opetitive behavior. The early 2000s witnessed the rise and rapid fall of many horizontal industry improving plays. While the fundamental concepts were extremely sound, that is, removal of internal inefficiencies around procurement for the above examples and associated leverage of scale, the desire to act as stand-alone entities that were revenue generators was not in synch with what the market was expecting and willing to accept at that time. As pure efficiency based horizontal entities, these ventures were extremely sound in both economics and theory.

We also present a new framework for valuation of the benefit streams that could emerge from widespread acceptance of industry changing horizontal or vertical entities that are either focused on providing a broad platform for a single process (back office) or a set of vertical processes (logistics and procurement) for an industry. This valuation mechanism allows us to put a valuation around the ability to sustain the benefit streams that are available for extraction. I have noticed too many companies focus on short-term benefits and revert to old cost basis since they do not fundamentally focus on changing the dynamics of their operations to deliver sustainable value for all constituents.

In conclusion, process extensibility to inherently shift the entire industry dynamics so that the entire industry structure benefits from streamlining and removal of redundancies. However, it requires careful planning and almost flawless execution since the number of impacted constituents is much greater in number than in the sole anchored situations.

* Portions of the previous two Chapters' were adapted from "The New Rules," by the author and published by Spiro Press, UK in 2002.

NEW MEASUREMENT FOR BUSINESS VALUE CREATION

NOTES FROM CHAPTER

UNSHACKLED PART III

The Top 10 Supply Chain Mistakes

No one disputes the economic impact of supply chain management. Study after study has linked supply chain performance to shareholder value and shown that total supply chain costs account for more than half of the finished cost of a typical product. But for the most part, initiatives to improve supply chain processes to date have fallen short of expectations. How else can you explain why inventory has continued to grow at a 3-percent compound annual growth rate over the last decade? And why 30-percent of new consumer goods products fail to meet basic financial returns?

Part of the answer may be that the execution of these programs is flawed or is inadequately planned by people who don't possess the right training and skills. I would also argue that ill many companies - certainly in those that I have worked for and with - there has been a tendency to treat supply chain initiatives simply as cost-containment or technology-implementation exercises. Finally, many efforts fail to realize their potential because companies view the supply chain only as the internal elements within their four walls. True supply chain management – what I call total supply chain management (TSCM) goes beyond the four walls. It begins and ends with the wants and needs of customers and consumers.

I have observed many companies struggling with their initiatives and have seen certain recurring mistakes - mistakes that if corrected could help companies realize total supply chain management. This, article condenses my experiences and observations, both as a practitioner and as a management consultant, into some guidelines that I hope can help others as they implement their supply chain initiatives. The guidelines are not meant to constitute an exhaustive list nor are they arranged in order of importance. Rather, they are simply a set of concepts, expressed as the mistakes that managers often make when attempting system-wide' change in their supply chains. I've focused on the ten most common mistakes I've seen in hopes that others can identify and avoid repeating them.

Mistake 1: Always viewing the supply chain as a "chain"

Dictionary definitions aren't always helpful. Merriam Webster, for example, defines a chain as a "series of things linked, connected, or associated together or a group of the same kind or function usually under a single ownership, management, or control." This definition, however, implies that a supply chain is a series of interrelated functions that have some coupling governance and are connected by a single process flow.

That view has worked reasonably well up to now. Traditionally, the supply chain has been partitioned into the "silos" of planning, procurement, logistics, and service, and many managers focused on extracting value from their own silos. For companies pursuing the early stages of change management - in effect, getting their own houses in order – this approach has delivered tremendous results directly to the bottom line.

But as further gains become progressively harder to obtain, companies need to rethink their supply chain perspective. Instead of viewing the supply chain as a series of functional activities, they need to see it as a process that spans across functions and organizations. On the surface, it may seem like a small change to ask for, but for many businesses, it has meant an overwhelming struggle. It's particularly difficult because it requires an outward focus. In addition to the traditional internal activities and relationships, supply chain practitioners now need to focus externally on business-to-business and even business-to-consumer processes and interactions. This change in focus requires new skills and training for many supply chain professionals as they now must now add external partnering to their skill sets.

The Top ten mistakes List

1. **Viewing it as a "chain"**
2. **Continuing to do business as usual**
3. **Having the wrong idea about control**
4. **Failing to synchronize demand and supply signals**
5. **Believing that technology is the real enabler**
6. **Failing to gain real visibility**
7. **Adopting a "One Channel Fits all Approach"**
8. **Misreading the people factor**
9. **Not leveraging global elements of supply chain operation**
10. **Underestimating the transformation task**

Companies in the early stages of this transformation may benefit from using a framework that takes a holistic view of the design-to-delivery process as opposed to the order-to-delivery mindset more typical of conventional supply chains. (See Exhibit 1.) It calls for listening to the design and external collaborative "voice" of the customer and tying marketing and consumer research into the supply chain. Using this framework to design the supply chain strategy, we can not only get the most out of the internal supply chain but also create a collaborative structure that allows for value creation between functional silos while keeping in mind the "total cost of ownership (TCO) structure."

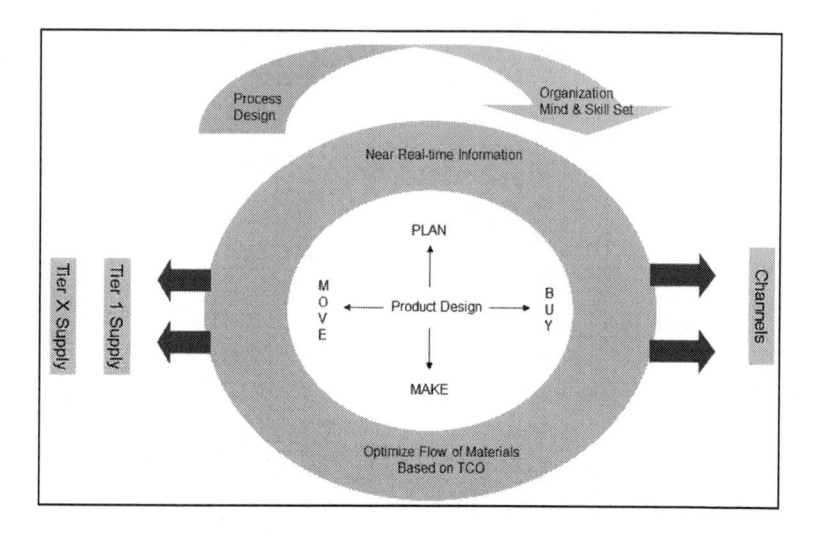

Exhibit 1: The Delivery to Delivery Framework

We have found that potential savings calculated in a siloed activity often subtract from optimal savings for the whole supply chain. The current wave of TSCM requirements is taxing companies whose domain or span of control is not well-defined and whose processes are focused on silo expertise and optimization, Already another wave is gathering, this one driven by retail channels working to slash system-wide inventory and total landed cost while keeping gross margin returns on inventory investment as high as possible, Companies that continue to think in "chain" terms as opposed to embracing the extended and dynamic supply chain will find this wave very tough to manage.

MISTAKE 2: CONTINUING TO DO BUSINESS AS USUAL

"Business as usual" is always an interesting concept. It keeps people within their comfort zones and lets business leaders avoid having to rearrange their market-facing strategies. The problem is that this stance can paralyze large-scale transformation initiatives that require fundamental changes in how the supply chain interacts with the rest of the business functions and in how the supply chain is positioned to take advantage of closer consumer interactions.

We find that companies that try to use their internal supply chain processes and metrics in their externally oriented and consumer-driven actions often end up failing to make the transition and impairing their internal processes at the same time. For example, the measurement around fill rates can be viewed as internal to the company or as an external metric for customers. But the business process that supports optimization of the internal fill rate is not the same as the one that can make it beneficial for the end customer. Forecasting processes that are focused on minimizing the error in product shipments from the factory or warehouse are not the same as the processes that utilize point-of-sale data to drive the supply chain.

Some years ago, I had a discussion about inventory turns and service levels with the supply chain chief of a global, multibillion-dollar consumer-goods company. Looking at turns improvement data from a range of peer companies, we discovered an interesting fact. Companies that did not substantially shift their go-to-market strategies or channel strategies achieved only small delta improvements as they traversed the inventory –vs. -service Pareto curve. (See Exhibit 2.) The classic example is Compaq vs. Dell. Compaq could make all the efficiency improvements it wanted, but unless the company changed its business model to the direct approach used by Dell-stripping out several operational layers in doing so-it could only realize incremental benefits.

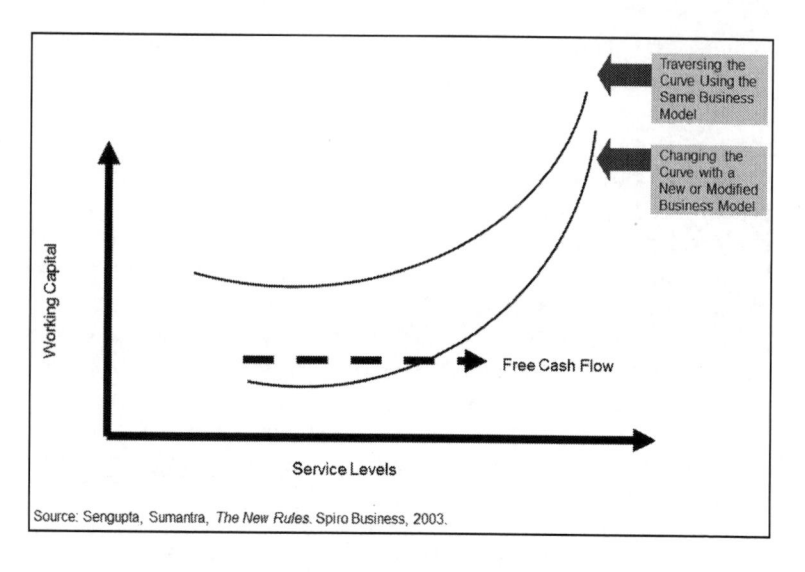

Exhibit 2: Moving the Business Curve

Mistake 3: Having the wrong idea about "control"

I've just finished reading *The Game Makers,* which traces the history and growth of Parker Brothers, the highly successful board-game maker. The era of mass production is highlighted well in the book, as is the fact that many companies brought repetitive commodity manufacturing in-house during the 1920s and 1930s to better control their own destiny. There is still a strong perception that virtual companies, or companies that have outsourced their non-core activities, give up some degree of control. Yet the connected economy is all about achieving superior results by leveraging the core competencies of alliance partners while maintaining a focus on your own strengths. A framework of leveraged value chains across an extended enterprise demonstrates the power of virtualization. (See Exhibit 3.) Not every company will be able to become virtual in all aspects, nor should they. Even a company like Cisco Systems-a wonderful example of an extended supply chain leader-still retains strategic control and planning of its overall supply chain and firm tactical control of key elements.

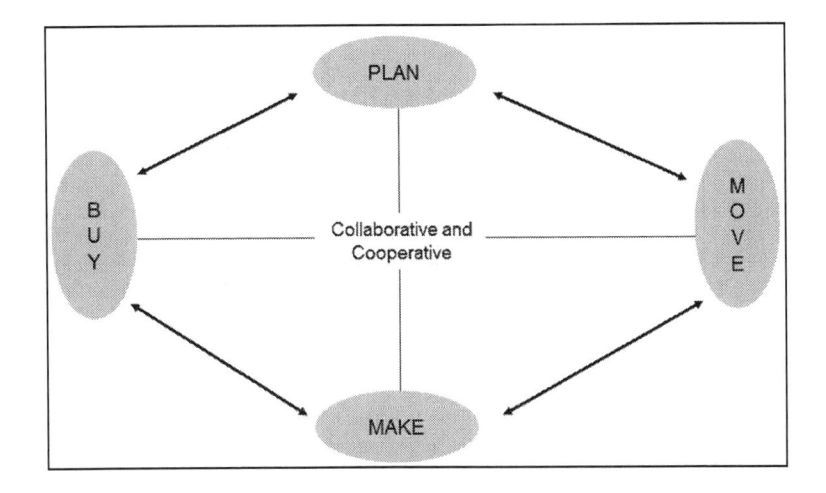

Exhibit 3: The Leveraged Value Chain

We've found that it makes economic sense to retain in-house control of the elements of the supply chain that add significant value to the customer and to partner with other companies for the commodity elements. In the future, supply chain success will be determined largely by the degree of partnership between the businesses that make up the extended value chain.

MISTAKE 4: FAILING TO SYNCHRONIZE DEMAND AND SUPPLY SIGNALS

Remember a few years ago, when Nike suffered significant financial problems largely because of a poor implementation of demand and supply planning systems and processes in its footwear division? 'Poorly synchronized demand signals and supply signals have created more problems with inventory availability across the supply chain than is reasonable. It boils down to the need to match financial forecasts with sales and marketing forecasts as well as with operations forecasts. In an age of scientifically generated baseline forecasts, the need to have three different numbers being generated by three different groups at three levels of details and using disparate data sources is nothing but a waste of good corporate resources and money. The companies that continue to pursue operational excellence by relying on shipment data are left with unproductive working capital and excess and obsolete inventory. They need to move closer to the actual point of consumption and migrate to using a single baseline forecast.

To some extent technology advances make it less crucial to constantly synchronize demand and supply signals. Leading-edge companies already excel at tracking point-of-consumption data as well as inventory at the last point of consumption, and they use sophisticated tracking technology to transmit the data effectively. As a consequence, their marketing functions can focus on building the brand and enabling effective promotions; sales can proactively influence customers' ordering pattern; and production, procurement, and distribution functions have one signal that is driven by customer data.

Mistake 5: Believing that technology is the real enabler

Six times out of ten, a complex supply chain project will involve an IT implementation. Someone once said that every business event triggers an IT event. This is absolutely true and the challenge lies in recognizing that, while a robust technology platform is necessary, it is not the sole condition for overall program success. It is all too easy to get caught up in "the SAP project" or "the Manugistics project" and to forget that the real change comes from the transformation of the business process to which the technology is being applied. And it's easy to forget that it is the dependencies between the supply chain silos, which really make transformations work. These may seem like subtle distinctions, but they have powerful and long-lasting repercussions. The optimal scenario is the confluence of the right people with a robust technology platform, which enforce and adapt a business process that supports the corporate strategy. The least effective scenario for a business transformation? An obsessive focus on and fine-tuning of the technology platform alone.

Mistake 6: Failing to gain real visibility

Plenty of supply chain managers want to improve supply chain visibility and to have their organizations more effectively act on the real-time information updates that are crucial to better visibility. But few have found a way to turn their wishes into practice. Every supply chain has inherent latency; it can only operate as fast as the slowest machine or process. The practitioners of effective SCM always seek to achieve visibility in ways that balance the burden of data collection with the benefit of reacting in real time. We recommend the use of the term "near real time" as opposed to real time. That perspective works well, for example, in gathering inventory data at the store level to run an effective vendor-managed-inventory program with channel partners. While it may be desirable to collect the information daily, it's more practical to do so once a week because the latency in all transportation networks is about three days (two days to deliver and a day to pick and pack), This not only minimizes total cost of the infrastructure but also allows the supply chain function to maintain some inherent stability in its various schedules.

We have found that enterprise resource planning (ERP) systems offer a *de facto* degree of visibility in the transaction, or order, side of the business; after all, ERP is an "enterprise recorder" of data. But many companies make the mistake of not going to the next step. And as a result, they end up data-rich and knowledge-poor. The principle I've often used is that all order transaction data, as well as production and logistical schedules, need to be available with almost zero latency. When piped into supply chain planning tools, the data can then be analyzed and interpreted as useful knowledge. Too many companies have fallen into the costly trap of assuming that the right ERP package from the right vendor would take care of things.

There's a parallel point with the introduction of radio-frequency identification (RFID). The RFID story has produced such hoopla that you could be forgiven for thinking that you're behind the curve if you don't have an RFID pilot project well under way. The latency argument applies here too. My key point here: Rich quantities of real-time data aren't universally beneficial. It is important for companies to identify where in their extended supply chains such data can be of business value.

Mistake 7: Adopting a "one-channel-fits-all" approach

For most companies today, there is no such thing as *the* supply chain - as in the *one and only* supply chain. In practice, there are multiple supply chain designs to suit the characteristics of the products and the channels they are sold through. The distribution channel isn't usually top of mind for supply chain managers. But if supply chain management is to be done right, it must extend all the way through the front office to the customer.

Many companies continue to struggle with integrating the supply' chain's many functional silos under a common organizational and reporting structure. They also have difficulty identifying metrics that tie all the functions into a loosely coupled entity. It's common to apply the same supply chain techniques-planning, procurement, logistics, and so on-to all products and channels. But it's a mistake to do so. I often refer back to a seminal article in the field of supply chain management by Marshall Fisher titled 'Which Supply Chain Is Right for Your Product." Fisher's article provides an excellent framework that uses product and channel characteristics to help determine the mode of operation for a supply chain. It's even more important to get that right these days as companies mix product portfolios that often have quite different characteristics. For example, they mix products with short lifecycles, such as fashion clothing or consumer electronics equipment, together with replenishment-based products that have long shelf lives or stock products with build-to-order products.

The "portfolio mix" trend really calls for multiple supply chains. The most practical way to run them is to determine the points of commonality across all the chains-where there is channel convergence or logistics convergence, for example and then to consolidate that function as a shared service across multiple product lines. The arrangement can still permit localization and separate management for the disparate functions. However, it does create the challenge of decentralizing a previously centralized function. Creating the right cost structure for each supply chain requires some out-of-the-box thinking as well as organizational constructs that don't fit with conventional logic.

Mistake 8: Misreading the people factor

How many times do we gripe that our employees aren't adapting to the new business model or that they're using new tools and processes in the same ways that they used the old ones? The "we've always done it this way" mindset is the leading reason for why many supply chain transformations fail miserably.

The traditional change-management approach involves plenty of training and attempts to teach individuals new skills so they can carry out their new responsibilities properly. Those efforts are necessary, but they're not enough. The traditional approach must be modified to suit the reality that not every individual will imbibe the new training and acquire the skill sets that management wants them to have.

In my experience, the biggest challenges for employees center around rigorous analytical thinking and technology understanding. Some people are just not temperamentally inclined to such thinking; many others lack the technical education to operate in the new mode. The results are discomfort for employees and disappointment and irritation for managers. Unless dealt with swiftly, the situation can cause widespread damage' to a transformation effort.

I often segment employees into four categories: (1) the early adopters who love change, who "get it" and very much want to be part of it; (2) the opportunists, who'll go along with a transformation initiative if there's "something in it for them"; (3) the followers, who will wait until change is well under way before they jump on board; and (4) the recalcitrant, who either don't get it or don't want to get it and will fight the change initiative all the way. (See the human adaptation pyramid in Exhibit 4.) It's vital to identify who will help with the supply chain transformation effort and who will hinder it. With that information, you can make informed choices about roles and teams in ways that will greatly increase the chances of a successful transformation.

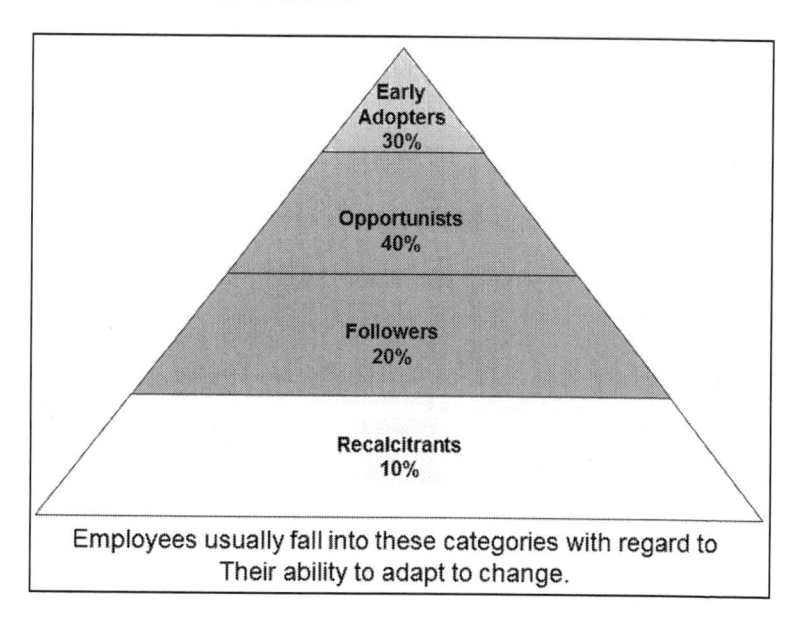

```
                    Early
                   Adopters
                     30%

                 Opportunists
                     40%

                   Followers
                     20%

                 Recalcitrants
                      10%
```
Employees usually fall into these categories with regard to Their ability to adapt to change.

Exhibit 4: The Human Adaptation Pyramid

MISTAKE 9: NOT LEVERAGING GLOBAL ELEMENTS OF SUPPLY CHAIN OPERATION

There's been much talk recently about the need to globalize the supply chain function as a shared service as opposed to a vertical model around geographies or business units. In other words, to have supply chain expertise available wherever and whenever it is needed around the world. It's an especially animated topic for companies that have global product brands (think Nike or Coca-Cola) and manufacturing that is globally dispersed and interchangeable. The topic has drawn plenty of attention because of its promise of significant cost savings.

For the most part, however, companies conclude that shared supply chain services won't work. But that's not necessarily true. In many situations such services make economic sense - particularly when it is possible to leverage expertise and volume across borders and to standardize the mechanisms that govern the ability to get product successfully to the customer. For example, companies can leverage global procurement even in the absence of global brands and global production. Globalization of supply chain functions and processes and shared leverage with partners appear to deliver productivity benefits of between 8 and 10 percent.

Moreover, shared services will be pushed further by major customers, whether suppliers like it or not. The message is this: We should not view the presence of global brands or the Cross-border movement of goods as necessary conditions for globalization of the supply chain. The reality is that globalization of the distribution channels may force us there anyway.

Mistake 10: Underestimating the size of the transformation task

It's easy to get carried away with the potential of an SCM transformation project and to overlook the interdependencies between the many efforts and process threads that make up the transformation. We also tend to pay too little attention to the multidimensional skill sets so vital to projects of such complexity.

Two best practices that we use effectively are the following: a long-term success horizon (three to five years) and dedicated project teams. We believe that an effective transformation typically takes more than two years, with many intermediate checkpoints and a range of metrics that must be closely monitored. We also believe that change cannot easily happen when people are only focused on and rewarded for their day-to-day roles. So we assign dedicated teams whose core job is to manage large transformations.

HEARING THE ORCHESTRA

In this chapter, I've tried to identify some of the main obstacles that trip up businesses as they attempt large-scale transformations of their supply chains. While several of the challenges I point to have been addressed elsewhere, I believe there is value in restating them collectively so that together they can become a catalyst for more forceful remedies.

The lessons here can be boiled down to two simple ideas. First, there is no "one size that fits all" approach to supply chain transformations- particularly given the growing complexity of the supply chain *and* of the customer. Second, there really are common threads around the pacing of change: applying sound human resource management, thinking outside the four walls of your internal supply chain, and managing your operations to a single signal-that is being driven by meaningful data from the end user. To emphasize: Supply chain transformation is indisputably difficult. But when all of the right concepts and actions come together, it is like listening to a beautifully composed and coordinated orchestra.

NOTES FROM CHAPTER

UNSHACKLED PART IV

Rethinking Supply Chain Planning

The rapidly evolving connected enterprise which extends from the suppliers' suppliers to the customers' customers-has three distinct characteristics: It is more connected than ever before, it is intricately interwoven with information, and it is decidedly global in nature. These characteristics have produced a new type of marketplace–one where near-real-time (or "zero latency") information is critical, where consumers increasingly interact directly with manufacturers, and where supply chain effectiveness swiftly translates to heightened competitive advantage and enhanced shareholder value.

Companies are under intense pressure to get a better product in the hands of the consumer, in the right quantity, at the right time, and for the right price. To do this, they are expending considerable time and resources on planning their supply strategy to respond to consumer demand. Yet traditional supply planning, once a sound and logical approach, is no longer enough. It takes too long and costs too much in terms of lost opportunity and suboptimal marketing and sales efforts. There's also the problem of the underutilized production, distribution, and material resources.

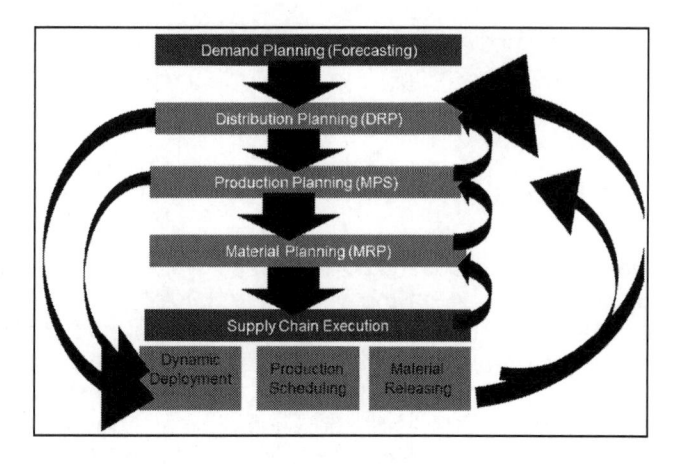

Exhibit 1: The Traditional Planning Process

This chapter addresses these issues. It presents a framework in which corporations will spend far less time on planning-while at the same time producing more accurate and dollar-optimal plans. The approach is called Constrained Resource Integrated Supply Planning, or CRISP.

This new methodology differs from conventional methods in a number of important ways. Traditionally, demand planning is followed by distribution planning, then by production planning, and finally by materials planning. (Exhibit 1 depicts the traditional planning process.) Yet this method results in plans that often are infeasible, un-reconciled with actual variables, and overly time consuming. By contrast, CRISP integrates the supply planning function and handling constraints and it does so earlier and simultaneously in the planning cycle. Early constraint management across the enterprise can improve the timing of marketing and promotional events significantly. This, in turn, enhances total sales volume.

Although the assumed end-goal of planning is revenue maximization, traditional planning methods hardly ever take into account the relevant enterprise cost levers. The result: A high potential for suboptimal, cost-intensive plans. CRISP avoids this trap by letting companies examine constraints simultaneously and meet the demand-while at the same time maintaining margin, optimally allocating funds and resources, more effectively 'planning sales/marketing events, and cutting supply chain costs.

The resources freed by this planning approach can be applied successfully to increase value-added services, collaborate more closely with the extended supply chain, mass customize, and create 1: 1 marketing over the Internet.

The Traditional Planning Environment

In the traditional scenario, companies devote days and sometimes weeks to the planning cycle, generating optimal plans for the different functional silos (marketing, manufacturing, distribution, logistics, and so forth). Yet although these plans may be optimal for each function, they are suboptimal- and maybe even infeasible for the enterprise as a whole. To give a practical example, a company might develop a feasible optimal plan for distribution. Yet that plan is rendered infeasible because it failed to consider the corresponding production plan, which indicated maintenance shutdowns or material shortages at suppliers.

As seen in Exhibit 1, in traditional planning, a forecast from the demand planning/ forecasting function (for example, sales or marketing) is sent into the unconstrained Distribution Planning (DRP) function, which then calculates the inventory balance and creates production orders for the Master Production Planning (MPS) Production planning then must verify whether sufficient manufacturing capacity exists for these production orders and then attempt to match demand with the available capacity.

The MPS sequentially sends the production quantities to a Material Requirements Planning (MRP) function, which generates the requisite purchase orders for procurement. This plan compares what has to be produced with the projected material availability. Only after the material plan is generated and found to be feasible can the supply plan be executed.

Throughout the process, information feeds back into the planning silos (the arrows in Exhibit 1), creating a complex matrix of information inputs, outputs, and loops. Thus, it is possible to develop a feasible distribution and production plan, only to have a material constraint render the plan outdated and infeasible.

In the conventional approach, the final plan sent to production scheduling goes through a series of three constraint checks or planning "gates." These checkpoints usually are operated by different people in different systems and perhaps within different organizational silos-thereby making the process all the more complex. Furthermore, these activities usually extend over several days, since each planning silo must do several iterations of the plan to arrive at a feasible and optimal solution before passing it on to the next silo.

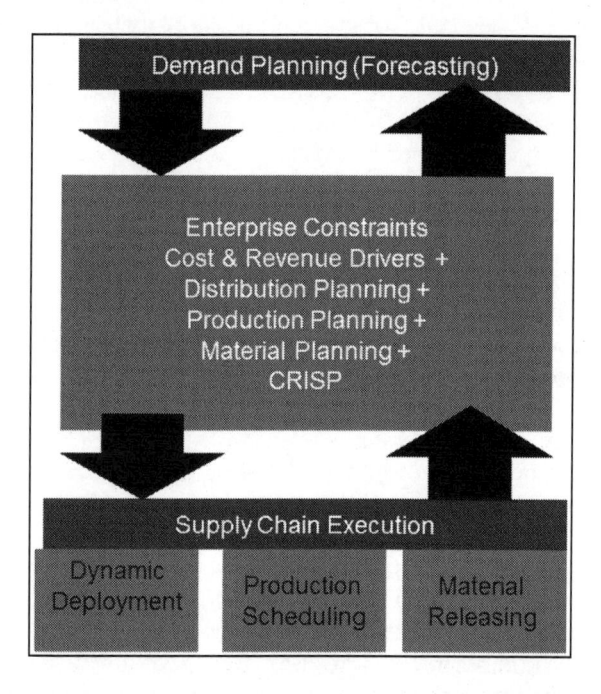

Exhibit 2: Planning Process Flow Using CRISP

CRISP: An Enterprise wide Approach to Planning

Compared with traditional planning approaches, CRISP can reduce planning time significantly while, optimizing the quantities and mix of products flowing through the supply chain. It simultaneously addresses all of the enterprise wide *supply chain constraints* (for example, production, supplier, transportation capacity), using supply chain *cost factors* (production costs, distribution costs, carrying costs, stock-out costs, storage costs, and so forth) and *revenue factors* (such as selling price, margin, profitability by customer, and strategic value of customer). This integrated planning approach leads to an improved choice, mix, and flow of an optimized and feasible supply plan through the chain's various links.

Exhibit 2 summarizes the schematic flow of information under CRISP. The graphic emphasizes the principle of integrated supply planning coupled with the early and simultaneous consideration of all the supply- oriented links of the supply chain. Using CRISP, the planner can constrain the plan for the entire chain to achieve an optimal supply chain solution.

The demand signal can consist of forecasts, orders, point-of-sale (POS) information-or a combination thereof. As shown in the exhibit, this demand signal is fed into the planning process. CRISP then constrains the demand with respect to the corporate objectives (for example, profit, cost, due date, and customer priorities) subject to numerous enterprise wide constraints (such as material, production, and distribution capacity). The constrained signal then is passed on to the supply chain execution function.

The constrained demand now contains information on key decisions such as procurement quantities, timing and quantity of build schedules, product mix, and outbound sourcing to distribution centers and customers. That broad capability extends well beyond the scope and range of traditional supply chain planning.

In addition, the constrained demand signal results in information about which customers will receive which products, how much they will require, and at what point. It also provides a complete profile of the facilities within the supply chain. Furthermore, order planning, dispatching, or third-party logistics systems can send order information to CRISP and initiate Available to Promise (ATP) or Capable to Promise (CTP) dates in a rapid fashion.

By taking time-phased costs and profitability into account, CRISP can help optimize the timing, frequency, and volume of promotions or sales events, thereby providing competitive advantage. The planning approach is particularly effective in determining the benefit/cost and timing of a marketing promotion or sales event.

It's important to note that collaborative planning through the extended enterprise can play a central role in transforming CRISP from a concept to reality. Collaboration between suppliers and customers complemented by strong internal collaboration will provide the comprehensive constraint base upon which to develop optimal plans. Collaborative efforts also will enhance the quality of data used.

They will result in better relationships between the links of the extended supply chain as that chain becomes more efficient and effective. In the connected enterprise, 1: 1 marketing will be feasible only when near-real-time planning can occur. CRISP is well suited to such marketing strategies since it allows the consumer to obtain an availability date or an Available to Promise number faster and more accurately. Also, the marketing and sales function can get a better sense of profitability from promotions after netting out supply chain costs.

DEFINING THE VALUE PROPOSITION

By gaining visibility over the various supply chain constraints early in the planning process, CRISP can increase the value of planning. The value proposition extends out to eight different activities, as depicted in Exhibit 3.

Sales/marketing promotional event planning: CRISP enables the sales and marketing functions to plan promotional events based on optimum profitability, while more accurately informing customers of what will be available and when. This capability allows the customer to plan events better and avert stock-outs. It also gives retailers and other OEMs added confidence in your organization.

Reduced planning time: CRISP communicates a plan based on a comprehensive supply profile to manufacturing, distribution, and deployment functions that is feasible and involves a huge reduction in the number of iterations. The end result: major time savings in planning activities for everyone.

Optimal product allocation: This new approach allows the supply team to allocate product to customers when there is not enough to satisfy all the demand. This feature also helps to rationalize the customer base and determine the cost of customer service by identifying the true cost and profitability of supplying different customers.

Optimal product mix: The plan considers product substitutions and category/product mix based on a comprehensive list of cost and revenue factors as well as enterprise wide constraints. The result is a profit-centric product mix. *Consumer response flexibility:* CRISP gives the planning functions greater visibility into enterprise wide supply chain bottlenecks earlier in the planning cycle-whether monthly, weekly, or daily. Increased visibility will enable them to plan more accurately. And it will improve the response time to consumer demand signals, while optimizing the supply chain.

Integrated optimal supply plan: CRISP develops a forecast that considers the major supply chain constraints across the enterprise-not simply in manufacturing or distribution. This approach ensures that you consider bottlenecks throughout the extended supply chain.

Enterprise constraint visibility: The CRISP approach enables the supply planning functions to alert suppliers and contract manufacturers to spikes in demand earlier in the planning process. This facilitates more proactive planning and collaboration, which helps to reduce stock-outs both at the supplier and at the customer levels. Taking time out of the business planning cycle frees up resources for other activities, improving the efficiency and effectiveness of the planning function

Profit/cost-optimized planning: Finally, CRISP drives the organization toward more profit/cost-optimized planning that is based on enterprise wide cost/revenue levers and constraints. In this way it facilitates achieving the goals of lower total operating cost, improving operating efficiency, and higher profits.

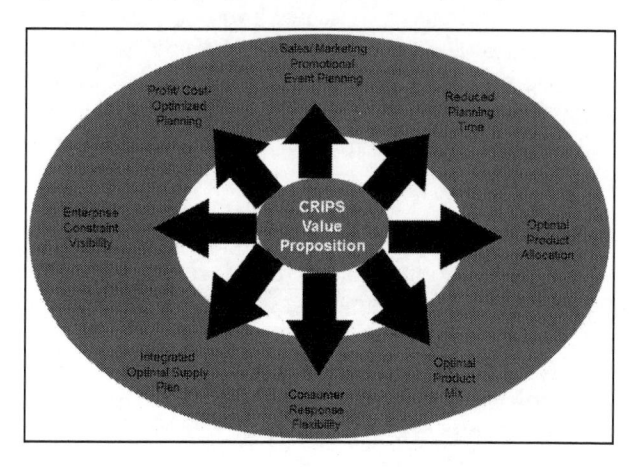

Exhibit 3: Value Proposition for CRISP

Five Components of a Successful Launch

With a sound knowledge of the value propositions, a company can begin the process of implementing the 'new planning methodology. The process begins by identifying the major components of the CRISP implementation.

Five of these are key:
(1) the strategic framework of the implementation;
(2) the impact on the organizational processes;
(3) the impact on the people who drive these processes;
(4) the tools and technology enablers; and (5) the core business knowledge that can brought to bear.
(Exhibit 4 depicts these key components.)

The discussion below underscores the individual importance of each component as well as how they interact. Combined, the components can deliver value in a comprehensive manner and at an accelerated pace.

Component 1: Strategic Framework

This component provides the blueprint for what is to come in the other four components. The strategic framework enables us to identify what will be required from each of those components. It also details the interactions that will occur between them during the implementation. A business should augment current adroit practices with other leading practices and benchmarks to develop an overall strategy and identify end goals.

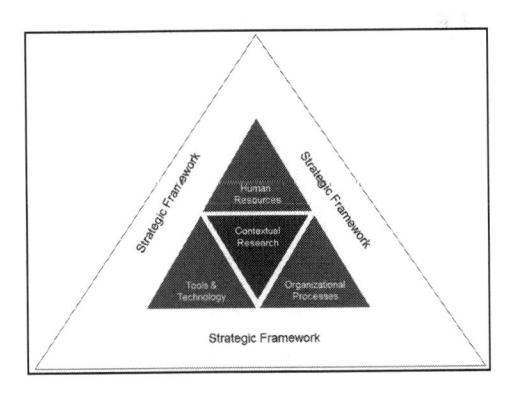

Exhibit 4: Core Components of CRISP Implementation

Understanding the strategic context of the implementation is critical. CRISP is but the first step toward "networking" or "consolidating" the extended supply chain. In examining this chain, CRISP deals with global demand and supply coordination. It then consolidates upstream, where the producer is collaborating with the suppliers. The extent of the integration is such that the boundary between the suppliers' plans and the manufacturers' plans seems invisible. This integrated process is replicated downstream between the customers and manufacturers.

The organization needs to be in a reasonable state of change-readiness to accommodate the significant process, organizational structure, and technological changes effected by CRISP. Because this new supply management concept will blur the lines between the different planning silos that exist today-taking down the "Berlin Wall" between departments, so to speak-executives need to be ready to handle the brief period of uncertainty (and maybe even chaos) that is bound to occur after a successful transition.

Component 2: *Organizational Process*

The organizational process component establishes the current state of the planning process, develops the future state, identifies the gap, and draws up an implementation roadmap.

The CRISP approach essentially mandates that the manufacturing, logistics, and procurement functions be seamlessly integrated to create the plan.

The integration can be accomplished in two ways: (1) realigning the organization so that all the planning silos merge into one larger silo or (2) coordinating the flow of information and actions so that the planning silos appear to be working as one virtual planning organization. The latter approach is the more difficult in terms of breaking down the internal barriers. Furthermore, competition for control may still remain, which could adversely affect the concept's quality, timeliness, and basic feasibility.

Importantly, professional performance goals and metrics should be tied to organizational performance metrics. Such alignment ensures that the CRISP initiative's participants are measured and rewarded against objectives over which they have some control.

Component 3: *Human Resources*

The human resources component considers the skill sets required for implementing Constrained Resource Integrated Supply Planning. It also addresses the change criteria and methodology needed for successful implementation. This component also encompasses organizational attributes such as role/job design, training and development plans, and measurements/performance metrics. The human resources component includes the communications plans between teams and departments as well.

For CRISP to work successfully, the people involved need to be well versed in all aspects of supply management (procurement, manufacturing, and logistics) as well as with the enterprise wide constraints and cost and revenue parameters. It is imperative to centralize as many planning functions as possible-or use cross-divisional synergy where centralization is not easily achievable.

Component 4: *Tools and Technology*

This component determines the optimum fusion of technologies to produce the best results. Throughout this activity, the organization needs to keep in mind that the overriding objective is to simplify and automate the planning process.

The plethora of supply chain technologies available today has resulted in some confusion for buyers. We have found that technologies designed to support the traditional supply chain planning silos are less likely to deliver robust CRISP solutions. By comparison, those developed to support simultaneous enterprise constraint management optimization are better positioned to support the CRISP methodology.

Component 5: Contextual Research

The contextual research component identifies leading practices in the industry, recognized benchmarks, and the organizations own experience in prior implementations of this nature. This represents the core of the organization's knowledge gained over time through past implementations and experiences. The contextual research enables the implementation to proceed at an accelerated rate because there are proven technologies, skill sets, and processes that can be drawn upon.

This contextual research component will form the basis of the performance metrics to be developed. Everyone involved in the integrated planning process must be working to the same metrics. To make sure that this hap1l~ns, top managements for all of the entities involved in CRISP must give their buy-in to the new planning approach and to the common metrics employed.

The Implementation Steps

The five key components are incorporated into the implementation steps discussed below. Note that the steps involve both process activities and technology enablers.

STEP 1: Strategy Design

In this phase we recommend a dual team structure. The first team determines the overall supply chain strategy and identifies key processes. The second team performs a value diagnostic to quantify the potential size of the supply chain opportunity derived from CRISP and to determine associated measurements. These activities set the savings/gains target. This step establishes the *Strategic Framework* and develops the blueprint that ties together the other components.

Key Step 1 deliverables include the overall strategy statement, a high-level design of all critical business processes, identification of the interrelationships among the supply chain initiatives, and senior management's sign-off on performance and process measures.

STEP 2: *Solution Definition*

During this phase, typically executed by the process team (the first team), focused assessment of current operations is performed and a future-state blueprint developed. Based on the blueprint, the team constructs an implementation strategy to determine appropriate rollout of the solution components.

It also sets the critical success factors and skill-set requirements for the *Human Resource* component. Along with the new performance metrics, the current-state and future-state assessments contribute to the *Organizational Process* component of the CRISP methodology. The process team also performs a gap analysis at this stage to identify any issues regarding the decision-support enabler, which contributes to the *Tools and Technology* component.

Key deliverables here include people and organizational environment assessment, current-state assessment executive summary, future-state flows for key processes, implementation strategy blueprint and related documentation, skill-set matrix, and gap analysis results.

STEP 3: *Solution Development*

The supporting decision-enabling software is tested and completed using a subset of the company's data. During this phase, the process owners establish and validate the detailed process flows as a part of the *Organizational Process* component. In addition, the CRISP-related roles/job descriptions are developed and candidates are identified to put into these positions. The *Contextual Research* component is used as a guideline to validate the process and identify the roles and responsibilities. The *Tools and Technology* component is applied in the pilot test of the technology (software) enabler.

Key deliverables include detailed process flows, data requirements, complete pilot models, and decision-support software configuration details.

STEP 4: *Solution Implementation and Post Implementation Support*

In this phase the pilot models are completed, and the process and technology move into production. All pilot models go through final process, systems, and user testing. Data are loaded into the database or models. End-user training is conducted. All project documentation is completed. The *Organizational Process* component requires implementing the new process structure and adhering to the new business process flows required by CRISP. The *Human Resource* component will make sure that the process

Owners actually take ownership of the new process and enforce both its usage and deliverable requirements. The owners also must coordinate with other teams as required by the process. Further, the *Tools and Technology* component requires that the software is used as prescribed.

Key deliverables in Step 4 include pilot rollout; end-user training; performance-measurement tracking; and process, system, and user testing. .

STEP 5: *Integration Architecture and Technology Environment Support*

All technical aspects are accounted for in this step, including data mapping, interface development, hardware and software installation, batch job development, and systems testing for the *Tools and Technology* component. In addition, IT training on technology is done for the *Human Resource* part of the solution. Further, the *Organizational Process* and *Tools and Technology* components jointly address any processor technology-interaction issues and identify possible resolutions.

Key deliverables in the fifth step include data mapping, technical architecture diagram, integration design, interfaces and batch scripts, and a data warehouse (if needed).

One Example of a Successful Implementation

In our work on Constrained Resource Integrated Supply Planning, we've discovered that this planning approach can improve operating efficiencies in a number of industry verticals. One recent CRISP application was at a bulk commodity chemical manufacturer with revenues in excess of $2 billion. The company's supply chain consisted of a multi-tiered network. More than 80 percent of the business was direct shipments; the other 20 percent went through the regular retail channel. Prior to embracing CRISP, the company had inventory levels in excess of 70 days' worth of supply.

The biggest challenge during the implementation was change management-that is, gaining consensus and free-flowing communication between the managers responsible for forecasting and inventory and the various trading partners. They were used to optimizing their functional silos as opposed to optimizing across silos with complete visibility into all enterprise wide constraints (demand, production, material, and so forth).

The successful implementation resulted in the development of cross-functional metrics and a well-defined Sales & Operations Planning process. The company continuously monitors the plan to make certain that execution and planning do not get out of synch.

CRISP improved inventory levels by more than 125 percent and freed up tens of millions of dollars in working capital. These expected benefits helped gain top management's approval to proceed with the implementation beyond that business unit.

The individual planning silos rarely take into account cost levers such as production, distribution, inventory storage, or customer-service costs. Nor do they typically consider revenue levers such as pricing or profitability by market or customer. Further, although local constraints (that is, those particular to the planning silo) are accounted for, enterprise wide constraints are hardly ever considered-much less accounted for. Enterprise-level constraints could include a critical material allocation for an industry or a multinational organization.

The following real-life example illustrates the problem with silo-oriented planning. In the early 1990s, two divisions of a consumer products company were planning the launch of their new product lines. Yet their independent planning processes failed to account for the fact that each was ordering a critical raw material from a common supplier. The supplier, who was constrained in the production of that material, had allocated product to the company as a whole, not to the divisions. But the divisions did not know this. Their silo-focused planning approach resulted in too much raw material being available to one division, and much too little for the other. Neither division realized that the material was available at the enterprise level and could have been easily transferred within the enterprise. The lack of integration resulted in a costly rescheduling of the product launch at the division.

The problems inherent in the example often result from divisional planning and incorrect alignment of metrics within and across the enterprise. And so, although the end plan may be feasible, it will probably not be the optimal plan from a profitability standpoint.

Avoiding the Pitfalls and Realizing the Potential

As with any new process that has significant potential to improve the business, CRISP also can be misused. Do not use or position this planning approach as a control mechanism over the many key areas of the business it will touch-like manufacturing, distribution, and materials planning. If people view CRISP this way, they will not cooperate fully with the initiative. And an uncooperative attitude on the part of the groups that provide constraint information to the CRISP planners will hinder the process, resulting in an inaccurate and ineffective plan. Lack of consistent and reliable data-coupled with uncoordinated updates-could, in fact, derail the implementation.

If these kinds of pitfalls are avoided, Constrained Resource Integrated Supply Planning can provide tremendous advantage to many industry segments High Tech, Consumer Packaged Goods, Retail, Automotive, Pharmaceuticals, Manufacturing, and more. It has the powerful potential to minimize supply chain operating costs and maximize profit across several business operations. CRISP can add significant value to the supply chain plan by helping to reduce time and increase cost efficiencies across the enterprise.

The CRISP approach is comprehensive in its constraint-management and optimization capabilities. As such, it is a valuable tool not only for the planning function, but also for sales and marketing.

CRISP is a flexible concept that can be implemented using a variety of decision-support software systems available today. The concept can bring great competitive advantage to any corporation that successfully implements it. Using the five key components for delivery of results-*Strategic Framework, Human Resources, Organizational Process, Tools and Technology, Contextual Knowledge-positions* the organization for a successful implementation.

As the marketplace evolves, corporations must become far more responsive to the consumer. How well they respond, in fact, will be the basis of sustained competitive advantage. CRISP lets you respond better and faster. This is a critical capability because as competition intensifies, supply chains increasingly will be competing against supply chains-rather than individual company against company. In this new environment, optimal cost/profit operations will be the prerequisite for prosperity and even survival. We end with a quote from Kevin Kelly's *New Rules for the New Economy:* "The new economic order has its own distinct opportunities and pitfalls. If past economic transformations are any guide, those who play by the new rules will prosper, while those who ignore them will not."

Unshackled IV was co-authored in Supply Chain Management Review in 1999 with Deep R. Parekh, Partner with Equus LLC. CRISP is a process construct and should not be confused with software products.

NOTES FROM CHAPTER

UNSHACKLED PART V

Planning for the Extended Supply Chain

Supply chain management is today considered a core function for every global corporation. The discipline has migrated from being a source of cost reduction to an enabler of high quality earnings as well as increased revenue.

However, certain global macro-economic factors have emerged in recent years that are forcing many corporations with well-defined and extended supply chains to rethink the construct of the core supply chain building blocks and operating model. These structural and economic changes include:

- Rapid globalization and convergence of the end customer/consumer channel with the supply base.
- Higher than normal escalation in commodity prices with shifting global supply.
- The advent of multiple capable and operationally excellent geographies with well-defined inbound and outbound logistics routes.
- Global availability of supply chain skills coupled with renewed focus on process standardization.
- Emphasis on the need to focus on one or two aspects of supply chain excellence to ensure global competitive advantage.

Core supply chain processes have often been described under the mega process umbrella of Plan, Source, Make, Deliver, and Return. This is part of the Supply Chain Operations Reference model (SCOR), developed by the Supply Chain Council. These mega processes will always constitute the building blocks of taking a product or service and delivering it to the end consumer.

However, the method by which a corporation defines the operating model and core process end state is what constitutes supply chain excellence.

I call the suggested method for defining the end state for the New Norm the "Five-S" Model. The five S's are *Structure* (physical and operating model); *Scope* (depth and breadth); *Span* (extent of the supply chain); *Scale* (degree of verticalization vs. virtualization) and *Skills* (availability and impact).

Companies need to rethink the core process across five dimensions To create a road map that will allow them to continue the journey of supply chain excellence. The article presents structured way for companies to rethink and align their supply chains to the shifting dynamics in the global marketplace. Many companies are proceeding in the journey. But from our perspective no one has achieved steady state or even close to the final design. It's not that supply chain executives have been resting on their laurels and have chosen to ignore the warning signs. Rather, it's more the speed and magnitude of the changes taken place.

The Structural Changes

Let's take a closer look at each of these structural changes:

Rapid globalization and convergences of the end customer channel with the supply base.

For at least 10 years now, the corporate world has been feeling the impact if globalization. Most corporations have developed or are in the process of developing growth strategies that are focused on serving the consumption and procurement power in the RIC (Russia, India and China) markets and the other emerging regions. These markets have very different consumption patterns and brand dynamics than those in the U.S. Buyers in these emerging markets tend to be more loyal to global brands and less focused on immediate gratification. Rapid globalization for top line growth had brought with it many supply chain issues surrounding the order to delivery (OTD) process. It is no longer adequate to treat the international business as an export activity, nor is it optimal to set up a completely self-contained OTD construct to serve the global markets.

As globalization has accelerated, there's been a convergence of the end customer with the upstream and original equipment manufacturers. This development is forcing all major companies to evaluate the impact on value added services and private label brands on the gross margins as well as on their go-to market strategies. Most retail and wholesale partners have launched their own private label strategies, which are requiring a shift in behavior from a focus on merchandising to one balanced with traditional supply and demand management issues that are faces by manufactures.

This is coupled with ever-increasing desire for post sales and value added services. On a recent tour of a few national retail chains, it was quite enlightening to see the huge emphasis being placed on value added services (for instance, Geek Squad from Best Buy) as well as the shifting mix of personnel skills that were needed to support these services.

Customer satisfaction is also a factor in this convergence. The early days of customer satisfaction, scores tended to focus on the customer as the channel partner. With the advent of various means of service transparency (such as Web sites, blogs, and message boards) it is just not enough to focus only on the "end of chain plus one" (where "ship to" is the end of the supply chain), but to also focus on the end point of product takeaway. However, many industries and global corporations still view the customer and consumer as two separate entities and offer varying degrees of service to both (as opposed to providing the optimal service to the point of product takeaway).

Higher than normal increase in commodity prices and the shifting nature of global supply.

In earnings announcements from CEOs and CFOs it's common to hear about increases in commodity prices impacting the quality of earnings or in many cases causing shortfall in net margin. Arguably, some of these companies use this as a crutch to mask sub-par top line growth. Yet there's a large element of truth regarding the increase in major commodity pricing over the last seven years. Some of this has been driven by the mismatch between demand and supply and by the rapid consolidation (and in some cases elimination) of alternate sources of supply. Corporations that have adopted best practices in procurement optimization and global sourcing are benefiting from favorable variances in key commodity prices.

Additionally, we are witnessing new supply sources opening up in the Middle East and Asia/ Pacific. This is coupled with increased availability of dependable logistics routes from these geographies, which makes the sourcing and manufacturing somewhat predictable within specified OTD lead times. However, as is often the case with leading edge innovation. Moore's law (which states that the industry standard integrated circuit doubles in complexity every two years), is being demonstrated by the global corporate ecosystem.

Advent of multiple capable and operationally excellent geographies with well-defined inbound and outbound logistics routes.

Recently, I had an extensive engagement in the Middle East for one of the region's largest retail chains. It was eye-opening to observe the product variations that were available from most of the major consumer products good companies there.

Operational excellence programs are also increasing in Asia and the Middle East, reflecting the Western influence. It is commonplace to hear about advanced concepts like category management, rapid replenishment, and dynamic pricing being applied within somewhat constrained or government controlled retail environments. Large scale ERP projects are underway across many of the large corporations in these regions as companies gear up to adapt their dated infrastructures (people, process, and technology) to the new growth scale.

Global availability of supply chain skills coupled with renewed focus process standardization,

North American companies long have maintained a heavy emphasis on supply chain management as they pursue the global growth agenda. In a similar fashion, European- and Asian-based companies have begun rapidly scaling their efficiency and operational effectiveness programs.

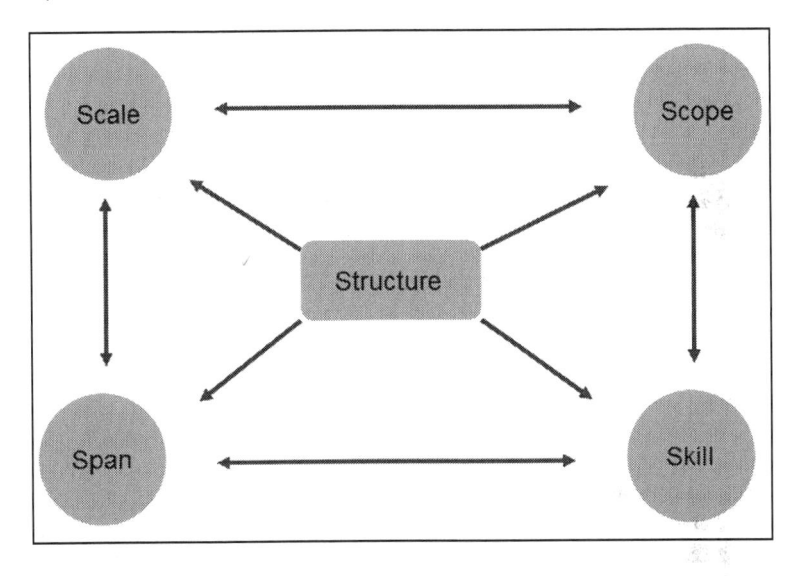

Exhibit 1: The "5s" Model

With the advent of globally available skills coupled with widespread availability "of established supply chain training programs, supply chain tasks are now routinely performed across the various SCOR dimensions in a truly distributed environment. In this way, traditionally mundane tasks such as data administration, analysis preparation, and post execution assessment can be performed with a high degree of quality across the globe. Additionally, analytically focused tasks such as planning and supply chain intelligence can be distributed worldwide to ensure multiple points of business continuity as well as rapid assimilation and dispersion of best practices.

Emphasis on the need to focus on one or two aspects of supply chain excellence to ensure global competitive advantage.

In the book *Myth of Excellence* the authors suggest that a company needs to be world class along select dimensions based on their core value proposition. It is almost cost prohibitive and virtually unnecessary to excel along all dimensions of the supply chain. I have always argued that every supply chain process should be subject to the "right sigma" as opposed to a blanket Six Sigma.

Companies need to think about more virtual supply chain models including potential "co-opetitive" partnerships, It is no longer cost effective or necessary to have an asset ownership model that involves complete control. Rather, the emphasis needs to shift to "virtual control."

All of the factors discussed above culminate in the need to reexamine the basic blueprint that underpins global supply chain models. And, as often happens, when the rules of the game change, we are faced with one of three choices:

1. Adapt the current model to the new realities.
2. Rethink the operating model to respond to the new realities.
3. Do nothing and see if the structural shifts are temporal or permanent.

The remainder of this article focuses on ways in which to implement the first choice, to build a new supply chain model that leverages the Five S's (structure, scope, span, skill and scale as depicted in Exhibit 1) and effectively uses the appropriate combination to transform and deliver a new supply chain.

Defining the Five S's

The Five S Framework extends the functional view of supply chain models like SCOR by factoring in the "how" (the executional aspect) to achieve necessary levels of excellence across all the functional dimensions. This framework is not intended to present a competing view of traditional supply chain functions, but assumes that most companies have adopted a variation of some supply chain process view that describes all aspects of the Design to Delivery (including reverse logistics) so that the various facets that merges the product, consumer, and informational elements of a supply chain can be tracked and traced (not necessarily optimized).

Structure (the fifth S) is the governing facet for the entire model that is built around the remaining four S's. Scope, span, scale and skill should be considered the foundational pillars of the executional strategy governed by structure.

While one could argue that the structural changes noted above have direct impact on every aspect of the Five S's, not all impacts have the same level of relevance on the restructuring of the supply chains. However, it is clear that the impacts will not remain static over a period of a time and will vary greatly by industry and associated product and growth strategies of a company.

I. SCOPE

The global scope of the supply chain is rapidly shifting focus from order-to-delivery to design-to-delivery. The walls between R&D for design and innovation, and customer service for pricing and returns are coming down.

It is no longer acceptable to have process, touch points that serve as handoffs between the functions with metrics that *serve* to optimize the individual processes. Companies that have heavy channel concentration within a type of channel such as do-it-yourself mass merchant, wholesale, or *B2B,* are rapidly reworking their supply chain constructs to focus on the end customer or customer back as opposed to product forward. This requires supply chain total landed cost metrics by customer and channel rather than by product only. Channel-specific decisions can then be driven to the right type of global supply chain – that is, one that has a cost and service metric that can be traded off to deliver consistent financial performance. This reflects the type of new thinking that will transform the supply chains from being horizontally focused to being globally driven by channel and customer metrics.

2. Span

Supply chains have evolved over the years from plant centric to product centric, and more recently to channel centric.

In most cases, however, the channel is a "bolt on" or afterthought addition to the supply chain. Very few companies have recast their supply chain to be customer back or "shelf back," where the shelf is the final point of product takeaway. Given the global convergence of channels coupled with information availability and visibility due to availability of content, it is becoming an unacceptable and expen*sive* value proposition to view any channel as just a store front for pre-designed products. channel-specific and promotions, along with the need for continued packaging innovation to maintain channel freshness, is forcing predominantly vertical supply chains to become more horizontally or channel aligned to respond to increased market demand.

In addition to the physical span being enlarged, the functional scope of the supply chain needs to expand from being focused on order to delivery to design to service. Key activities here might include the supply chain's close integration and active engagement with product commercialization and assimilation of the customer ser*vice* function as a major supply chain process.

3. Scale

A common problem that has corne up during many of my recent discussions with smaller companies that lack the production volume and scale is their need to execute with the same levels of supply chain sophistication as the companies that possess the needed critical mass. Here, our definition of scale deals with three aspects:

- Vertical and virtual models that is comprehensive across all assets including the *view* that a business process is an asset.
- The degree of virtuality that is appropriate to enable the corporation to maintain control over the relevant levers that are used as competitive differentiators.
- The type of virtuality that can be used to provide relevant scale even in a co-opetitive environment across the various supply chain processes and functions.

4. SKILL

The best strategies can often fail because of poor execution.

Further; over 50 percent of execution involves a high degree of human touch . The touches are executed by people of various skills-ranging from the execution-oriented supply chain skills needed across all the major CM processes to the right level of analytical, strategic, proactive, and reactive thinking. Just as we would manage a product portfolio, we now have to focus on managing and optimizing a people and skills portfolio that can be deployed globally and be used to drive seamless business process excellence across processes and countries. In a recent survey that we conducted among a dozen heads of global supply chains, skill attraction, retention, globalization, and training were singled out as the highest priority agenda items on the performance dashboards.

5. STRUCTURE

The culmination of the other four S's results in the final structure of the new supply chain. This structure needs to encompass the physical, functional and informational view of the supply chain so that tradeoffs can be made while designing the "right Five S model" that is based on product and, growth strategies. This is also the dimension

S number	Dimensions needed to define and execute
Scope – 1st	Process and P&L for Channel
Span – 2nd	Physical and Functional
Scale – 3rd	Virtual vs. Vertical; Type of virtuality and degree of virtuality
Skill – 4th	Mix and Type
Structure – 5th	Physical; Functional and Informational

Exhibit 2: Table Key Aspects of Each "S"

that determines the level of investments and retooling that is necessary to gain the right amount of traction and excellence that is required to adapt and flourish based on the relevance of the shifts. Exhibit 2 summarizes the various aspects and dimensions of the Five S's as we have outlined above.

Designing the Future Model

There is no silver bullet that a company can use to design future-state global supply chain. What is needed is a structured process rooted in the right mix of strategic guidance coupled with hard core analytics and blended with the right level of scenario modeling. Reorienting the supply chain is a strategic shift and should be vetted through a process that is closely aligned to the strategic planning processes followed in most large global corporations.

We recommend the use of a structured process that employs five tasks: Analyze, Map, Align, Educate, and Develop. Following this approach will help achieve the desired goal of creating a robust and sustainable future state operating model.

Analyze. It is always necessary to define the "universe" of factors needed to understand the dynamics of the industry and the speed of shift that can occur. One of the major factors that should be considered is the basic economic equation that governs every company:

CHANNEL PRICE (CP) = GROSS PROFIT (GP) + TOTAL LANDED COST (TLC)

We find that very few companies have a good grasp of the various components that make up CP or TLC. The debate often rages between the actual CP vs. the listed CP with the difference primarily being driven by the trade allowances, discounts and other SG&A related factors that are often hard to allocate back at the product and SKU level.

Similarly, many global corporations have yet to unravel the exact numbers behind TLC. Costs are often grouped under major categories such as material, logistics, and property. But the level of granular detail required to understand product and channel costs is lacking. It is extremely important to gain as much granular cost and pricing details so that informed trending analysis can be performed to enable fact-based decision making.

All economic analysis should be conducted as close as possible to the lowest common denominator. This is necessary to understand the basic cost and profit drivers that are being impacted by globalization as opposed to the cost/profit drivers that are internally sub-optimized.

Additionally, it is just as important to study the economics of the closest competitors as it is to understand the economics of adjacent products and brands, especially for the retail channel-focused corporations. Shelf space is the key constraint that all companies are fighting over, and the retail channel tends to perform their category profitability based on the entire set of products that serves the category. Store visits are a good way of understanding the category dynamics in retail placements of products that are in the same aisle or within close proximity of the aisle. Company managers who get wrapped around the axle of their own product categories often forget that retail gross margin return on inventory investment is extremely space-dependent.

The final variable in the analysis task relates to better understanding the efforts being pursued by the upstream and downstream channel partners (multiple tier suppliers and downstream finished goods processors or carriers). Cost and profit innovation is often occurring at the very ends of the consumption or the creation value chain since these companies are either closest to the consumption patterns or are the originators of innovation that creates processed product value.

Map. The logical follow-on is to map the major industry and adjacency drivers to the global structural changes discussed earlier in the article. Any additional changes can easily be added. This exercise provides the detailed relevance matrix. for the corporation that can be used to understand the emphasis areas across the Five S's.

Align. The next big task is to determine the most likely and least likely industry disruptive situations that could occur across the dimensions and their associated impact across the Five 8's. This *will* allow the corporation to create sustainable business plans that factor in the ends of the spectrum. Recently, there have been many instances of large global corporations facing product recalls (such as Mattel and Bausch and Lomb) based on a variety of factors. Corporations need to understand what their industry dynamics would be in extreme events (such as lost markets or lost partners), and the associated impact that would need to occur along the Five S's. For example, is the event such that the new scale would necessitate some long term structural decisions or skill redeployment? These are just meant to be illustrative examples of shifts that will trigger global supply chain redesigns.

Educate. Over the years, I've observed that the best designed strategies do not make it to execution due to the lack of education both up and down the organizational ladder. Many corporations tend to minimize the amount of change management and communication planning that is required to effectively execute strategic and structural supply chain shifts. I cannot overemphasize the need and importal1ce of such activities.

However, I would also caution against turning these efforts into a "change management circus" that attempts to educate and achieve consensus among every single person in the organization. It is probably sufficient to focus on the top 20 percent of the highest influencers and the naysayers. Then allow for information seepage and dissemination that occurs as a result of the halo effect from that 20 percent.

Develop. The final step in designing the future operating model is to develop the capabilities required to execute and Sustain the to-be state. The word "capability" is key in this since it implies that these efforts need to encompass plans that should cover impacts to people, process, technology, and associated metrics or measures.

The development of capabilities is explained below.

IMPLEMENTING THE MODEL

Implementing a supply chain is a highly complex task in its own right and it is further complicated by the inherent change management effort needed to help employees unlearn new ones.

One of the largest stumbling blocks is the passive-aggressive behavior that is exhibited by the "middle of the pack" people, not the top or bottom performers. Implementation effort of this type should include detailed design and plans along several dimensions.

The detailed decomposition and realignment of processes that need to be updated, changed or added should be carefully crafted if the execution is to be successful. This applies not only to the core SCOR-related processes that need changing but also the ones that are covered by the second S, Span. Often during implementation, companies forget that they have conditioned the channel partners to enable their inbound/ outbound processes to align with the company (remember, span overlap occurs on both sides of the value chain). It is also important to use the 80/20 rule while unraveling the process maps – focus on the 80 percent that is relevant and adds either competitive advantage or is needed for regulatory compliance.

Companies must do rigorous process redesign to ensure that users can apply the analysis and documentation with minimal extra work load. This is essential for the success since resources In general tend to have their workloads optimized based on the current processes.

Most redesign efforts also entail an alignment shift and augmentation of existing skills in the organization. However, given the global shifts we have found that some skill augmentation for analytical rigor is often required to create real-time information from a large quantity of new data.

This would include skills such as operations research and advance statistical analysis as well as lean and Six Sigma capabilities. Additionally, preparing the supply chain organization to migrate from a "batch centric" orientation to a "flow centric" one requires careful thought and implementation.

While technology components should never be at the forefront of a redesign effort, more than 80 percent of such efforts typically require the use of technology and automated enablers to ensure sustainability. The total solution should include the infrastructure and application linkage-related items that are necessary for end-to-end system and process enablement. While system-wide compatibility continues to be an issue, it can be managed with the use of automated tools. System-wide security and disaster recovery plans often require updating.

My firm belief is that human beings are rational and act as they measured and incentivized. Hence, in order for the effort to be successful and sustainable the necessary, appropriate measures and Incentives must be in place. These would include clear cross-functional accountability, a focus on Continuous improvement and executive ownership of business benefits (cost and revenue).

Additionally, we recommend that the champions in the organization should ensure the appropriate system-wide visibility across the impacted process and functions as necessary.

While there is no magic formula for success, we have found that every implementation involves elements of all of the factors discussed above and should be executed in multiple steps and iterations. It is important to adopt and learn in this process since most companies are charting new dimensions in their operating model. It is not possible to get everything right the first time around via the old "big bang" approach. Or, as one of my colleagues reminded me, we are running a marathon and not a 100-yard dash.

Critical success factors

It is next to impossible to guarantee success of any initiative. However, there are a set of common pitfalls that we will highlight that will enable a greater success rate for the transformational effort. These are along the same dimensions that we used to describe the implementation plan - that is, Process, People, Technology, and Metrics.

Process Success Factors

1. Design a process to be lean and yet flexible. Too often we optimize the process to the point where it becomes tough to change and adapt for future shifts
2. Design for the 80 - 20 rules; i.e. as long as, 80 percent of the issues are addressed, the process will adapt over time for the remainder. It becomes unmanageable and overly complex to design for every possible nuance
3. Use the "adopt and go" philosophy. Do not try to plan the implementation in so much detail that it takes forever to gain the desired benefits instead focus on the learning aspect from every iteration since many of the variables tend to shift during the process.
4. Design for global commonality as much as possible

People Success Factors

1. Focus on deploying the right mix of strategic, tactical and executional based skills in order to achieve the desired results.
2. Pay careful attention to the training and retraining of the individuals so that the skills are sustainable
3. Globally identify and deploy the resources with a focus on distributed process management and optimization

Technology Success Factors

1. Monolithic applications and deployments are a thing of the past and should be avoided at all costs.
2. Emphasize the global accessibility and scalability of all efforts even if there are multiple instances and environments in play - the future calls for consolidation and global distribution across processes and functions
3. Repeatable deployments should be planned so that deployment costs and times reduce with every iteration
4. Maintain a high level of discipline on the level of customizations that are performed to minimize total cost of ownership.

......and the final success factor is MEASURE; MEASURE AND MEASURE everything so that visibility and accountability remains at the forefront.

NOTES FROM CHAPTER

UNSHACKLED PART VI

Multi Channel Management of Supply Chains

The 3.0 era has arrived and taken the world of commerce by storm. Companies ranging from the *Fortune* 500 and Global 2000 to small independent businesses are working, aggressively to avoid getting disintermediated, reintermediated, or otherwise obsoleted by this remarkable new technology.

Every company in every industry is feeling the Internet's effect. But one segment where the pressure is particularly intense is retailing. The traditional bricks-and-mortars are struggling with how to create an Internet presence that leverages - not devastates - the mainline business. In essence, these companies are seeking the governance model for a new type of business called "click and/or walk." Consumers can buy and return goods from these hybrid entities either by clicking online or by walking into the front door of the store and they can do both.

Retailers have taken differing approaches to the evolution of the click and /or walk construct. Some have tight integration in the merchandising and back office functions while others tend to maintain a few degrees of separation between the front end retailing and back end support to allow for mass personalization. However, all retailers and e – tailers agree that consumers are seeking tighter integration between the two entities for issues such as product returns; product servicing as well as customer / consumer help services. Hence the days of attempting to create separate physical and financial structures that are stand alone, seems to be a phase from the days of internet euphoria or maybe as some call it, Web 1.0.

As they work to develop their click and/or walk strategies, however, most companies are sub optimizing their assets. The main reason for this relates to the revenue sharing and cost-allocation models used to reward and/or penalize shared participation in process, content, and commerce-one of the fundamental underpinnings of the governance model.

Specifically, most companies are applying traditional fair share allocation schemes based on volume or revenue that are inadequate and inappropriate for the Internet-enhanced businesses of the 21st century.

This chapter provides three alternatives (going from complete separation to full integration of intellectual and physical assets) for revenue propagation and governance of the click and/or walk enterprise.

These options are:

1. *Separate and Operate-The* physical and online businesses are operated as two separate entities under this option.

2. *Share and Operate-Under* this approach, some key services are shared, and some common metrics are used across the two businesses.

3. *Joint Operation-This* option finds the physical and online units integrated and operated jointly. The business has a well-defined revenue propagation mechanism that optimizes the participation of both business units. It also considers the intangible effect of factors like brand leverage and the flexibility to adapt to new and emerging business models.

The application of our framework will accelerate the emergence of click and/or walk organizations. In fact, it may well be that these enterprises will dominate the face of business-to-consumer (B2C), business-to-business (B2B), and consumer-to-consumer (C2C) commerce for the foreseeable future and this could result in significant wealth creation for the stakeholders and more choices (but maybe not lower prices) for consumers. Yet the click and/or walks must move forward decisively. Wall Street has a way of penalizing indecision with low market capitalization.

The Landscape Today: Invasion of the Pure Plays

A plethora of Internet pure plays have created an online presence with the hope of disintermediation of the traditional retailers. Two of the best-known examples, of course, are Amazon.com and Buy.com. All of these companies share a common vision of making online shopping easy for the end-user through a large selection of merchandise, ease of navigation and browsing, and hassle-free shopping from the comfort of one's own home or office.

Oftentimes that vision has been clouded by the harsh realities of having to fulfill customer orders on time and with close to perfect service. As realities set in, the original online concept of totally disintermediating the retail sector begins to appear highly infeasible-and the e-tailers have had to change their expectations accordingly. An example of shifting business strategies is provided by Amazon.com. At its conception, the start-up's goal was to be an infomediary and sales agent with no ownership of product or final delivery. However, since Amazon.com also wanted to provide superior customer service, that initial model was abandoned for a hybrid one-a model that included the addition of 3,000,000 square feet of warehouse space spread across multiple distribution centers.

The traditional bricks-and-mortar companies like Nordstrom, Best Buy and others have decided that the perceived disadvantage of having physical stores actually can be converted into a competitive edge. For their online business, they believe, the physical assets can be leveraged to handle fulfillment and product returns more efficiently while at the same time cross-promoting the brand name. The challenge that these established retailers face as they move into the online world, however, is what governance model to use in their new click and/or walk businesses.

A number of approaches have been tried to date. A company like Nordstrom.com, for example, seeks to leverage the parent firm's credibility, brand awareness, customer loyalty, vendor relationships, and existing store and distribution infrastructure. Nordstrom management has articulated such goals as "to serve the customer wherever they want to find us" and "to provide a seamless continuum of shopping experiences across all distribution channels." In the future, Internet customers may be allowed to locate special items that are not available online but may be found in the stores.

Another emerging click and/or walk leader is Best Buy. This company's online business plans to leverage existing Best Buy retail stores for Internet returns, advertising, promotion, and warranty. Both the physical and online entities also will engage in brand awareness and cross-promotion initiatives. In fact, the company's CEO has been quoted as stating that the synchronization of the consumer experience among all of Best Buy's channels-retail stores, catalogs, and the Web-ultimately will be the company's most powerful offering.

The Best Buy and Nordstrom examples show a high level of cooperation and coordination between the physical and the online operations. Yet there are many more examples of companies that have not reached that level. They are sharing infrastructure in some cases and, in other cases, not. In still other instances, organizations are adopting a mixed strategy consolidating some functional areas between the physical and online businesses while keeping others separate.

These diverse examples reflect the complexity involved in determining the infrastructure sharing, delivery channels, and process content that is optimal for wealth creation of both the online and physical enterprises. We have found that approaches vary with pre-existing business conditions. That is, some companies can make the transition from physical only to click and/or walk simply by adjusting their existing business practices to accommodate the new sales channel organization. Others need to redesign the business models from the ground up.

No approach has been found to be clearly superior to any other. Wall Street analysts have discussed the tremendous online potential of bricks-and-mortar retailers. At the same time, the analysts are cautioning traditional retailers that they must capitalize on this potential in a coordinated fashion in order to contain costs. But interestingly, the stock market has provided neither notable punishment nor strong reward for any of the companies making click and/or walk plays.

Many of the retailers appear to understand the benefits of consolidating certain functions as they develop their click and/or walk strategy. And some have implemented consolidation or shared service solutions. Few, however, have communicated effectively the strategic intent of their retail and dotcom growth either to the management of the two entities or to Wall Street. This not only causes distrust and confusion among executives but also leads to market capitalization fluctuations. It's interesting, by the way, to see some of the retailers creating tracking stocks for their online business. The logical inference is that at some time in the future they will create *two* separate business entities, which brings into question how much synergy will remain.

Three Options for Click and/or Walks

The governance options for click and/or walk corporations span a continuum from total independence to optimized use of shared services and joint ventures. To date, no option has emerged as the clear-cut choice for click and/or walks to follow. It should be noted, however, that some companies have experienced erosion of market capitalization because of a perception that the mainline business is continually subsidizing the online operations.

The three options presented here go across the spectrum of asset leverage - from complete separation of the click and the walk worlds to a close integration of the two. Exhibit 1 summarizes the degree of separation for the three options along the key components of physical infrastructure (stores, distribution centers, fulfillment hubs, administrative space); information (systems, data, and market intelligence); and process (business planning, back-office functions, relationship management and so forth).

Option I: Separate and Operate

The simplest solution is the separate and operate option, in which each entity operates as a self-funding line of business. The parent corporation can either choose to relinquish control of both organizations or remain on the boards of both.

Options		Physical	Information	Process
	Separate and Operate	H	H	H
	Share and Operate	M/H	M/H	M/H
	Joint Operation	L/M	L/M	L/M

Degree of Separation: H= High, M= Moderate, L=Low

Exhibit 1: Degrees of Separation

The equity allocation is defined for each organization in a manner that allows for aggressive recruiting and retention of key talent for both operations. The physical infrastructures and other fixed capital investments are adjusted for a onetime split allocation by both corporations as line items on the P&L (profit and loss). The same is true for the investment in working capital for both companies.

In this option, each organization maintains its own accounts payable process and infrastructure as well as its own information technology, business planning, merchandising, and supply chain operations units. External facing activities such as customer relationship and trading partner alliances are handled individually as well.

There are some advantages to this model. One is that each entity controls its own destiny, which often is perceived to be a prerequisite for any dot-corn's eventual success and profitability. Another is the ability to make and execute key decisions in

"Internet" time without having to plow through a cumbersome corporate bureaucracy. Costs are allocated fairly easily except for the one-time adjustment in fixed and working capital. This one-time allocation can be performed by using static growth projections of revenue, lines of business, and projected SG&A (sales, goods, and administration) costs.

But there are disadvantages to the separate and operate model, too. Our analysis of some of the major click and/or walks shows this option to be the most expensive. This is due to duplication of management structure, reduced system compatibility, uncoordinated supply chain activities, lack of merchandising leverage, higher levels of working capital, and inadequate leveraging of brand equity.

Option 2: Share and Operate

A middle-ground option often is the share and operate arrangement between the bricks-and-mortar company and its online counterpart. This approach brings to bear some well-established and key operating philosophies-namely, shared services for key activities and the effective use of metrics to drive consensus. Shared services is not a new concept in industry (consider, for example, the outsourcing of shared information -technology services). It's also common in the financial sector for items such as check clearing, printing, and accounts payable. Recently, new companies have emerged that provide asset-based services for large-scale distribution. These services have proved attractive to small and medium-sized retailers seeking to share logistics services between the online and physical entities.

Some of the key activities that can be shared under this model are accounts payable, information-technology services, and supply chain execution support. The two organizations retain a high degree of independence with regard to the physical infrastructure and supply chain planning. However, some physical store leverage may be used, such as in-store kiosks that attract customers to the online brand or joint advertising by the two businesses.

A big advantage of the share and operate model approach is the focus and accountability that each corporation brings to its business and supply chain planning. There's also greater compatibility, of information flow to and from the end-consumers as well as better management of working capital.

As the degree of shared services increases with this option, however, so does the difficulty of cost and revenue allocation that goes hand in hand with asset leverage. A convergence of three, major activities needs to occur to provide the appropriate leverage of assets for both the physical and online entities.

These are:

- Activity analysis-A fairly detailed and dynamic activity-based costing analysis of the shared activities needs to be performed. Particular attention must be paid to the inherent differences between handling of bulk vs. multiple smaller order quantities. Also, the physical layout of the key pick, pack, and ship facilities tends to be significantly different for the online vs. the offline world. Accordingly, all of these activities need to be analyzed carefully as well.
- Scarce-item allocation system-An optimized scarce and excess inventory allocation and adjustment system must be developed that takes into account total landed cost, business growth, customer priorities, channel priorities, and historical usage rates of the units. This allocation method protects the smaller business (typically the online corporation) from being shortchanged when items are in heavy demand. It also protects them from having to bear the cost of higher investments in working capital required of the physical corporation.
- Metrics-The activity analysis and scarce-item allocation system are used as inputs to the third critical activity-developing metrics. Time and time again, we have found that compensation-related metrics drive executive behavior. Where joint modes of operations are involved, the metrics for senior executives need to be tied into the overall well-being of the entire corporation while at the same time maintaining

a healthy balance for the individual P&Ls. Metrics used to foster shared success effectively are cash-to-cash cycle time, order-to-delivery response time, total delivered cost, delivery performance, and return on assets. These metrics, among others, can serve as an "executive management measure" that would be reviewed on a frequent basis to ensure the asset leverage.

Option 3: Joint Operation

Much has been written about how some bricks-and-mortar corporations with a high degree of brand equity have been able to turn the asset disadvantage into a distinct competitive differentiator. In fact, Wall Street analysts, investment bankers, and financial advisors are predicting that the companies that are able to optimize the leverage of their assets (physical and intellectual) will be the eventual winners. The third option, which we have termed *joint operation,* most closely approximates that paradigm.

The optimized use of assets' in this option involves a high degree of shared services between the two corporations. Then shared services or joint operations include information technology, physical assets (such as using stores for order fulfillment and reverse logistics, co-branding and promotion, and joint promotion planning), intellectual and process capabilities (like vendor relationship management, inventory and deployment planning and execution, merchandising, and marketing), human'-resource functions, and all back-office capabilities. The effective joint operation of these activities will result in superior customer experience both online and offline. Importantly, it also will lead to a higher return and wealth creation for the shareholders.

It is possible to use a framework similar to the share and operate model for this joint option. However, the share and operate framework is not the best method of executing asset cost and profit-sharing allocations. A more rigorous approach typically is required to eliminate subjectivity from the process. Such an approach also can be applied to assess the allocations in the horizontal trading exchanges.

The joint operation approach attempts to ensure that when an entity takes a cost increase in its P&L statement for the betterment of the entire corporation, it is compensated accordingly. All other cost-allocation methods, such as fair share and usage rates, ignore the issue of motivation-that is, why the corporations or participating functional group should accept an allocation that exceeds its independent opportunity cost.

The joint operation methodology is composed of four phases:

1. Joint permutation analysis. This first phase involves estimating a joint cost function for all the possible permutations of corporations that are sharing assets either online or offline. In the case of exchanges, this would include all participating companies. The joint cost function for a permutation is the least total delivered cost of serving all participants in that permutation. The guiding idea behind this activity is to share the cost when all participants work-together.

2. Joint incentive plan. Phase two involves the design of a joint incentive plan, in which, all entities participate. This incentive plan treats everyone equally in the event of business upswings and downturns. In other words, we need to ensure that the sum of all cost allocations equals the joint cost function for the corporations, and that for every possible permutation the sum of individual allocations is less than the joint cost function for that permutation. The rationale for this is simply to ensure that no participant is charged more than its stand-alone cost.

3. Business validation. In phase three, we ensure that the allocation scheme satisfies some basic business principles. This means making certain that cost functions add up from an accounting standpoint and ensuring that as participant contributions to all permutations increase or decrease, the allocations remain proportionate. It also involves ensuring that the allocations are viewed as universally fair so that no participant would need to renegotiate because of fluctuations in currency values or future hedges.

4. End-goal computation. In phase four, the actual allocation of the costs can be computed by using a variety of methods. One method that works well when corporations are signed up in random order is to determine the incremental marginal cost of being included at the moment of signing up or being included in the joint operation venture. In this method, the marginal cost is the total cost of that corporation (in an e-market, for example) or a function (in the case of two corporations) relative to the entire participating group.

Back to the Fundamentals

In helping companies apply the options described above, we have found that the separate and operate approach is the most expensive. In fact, its cost runs approximately three times as much as that of the joint operation option. The share and operate approach provides a middle ground from a cost standpoint. Yet it often proves cumbersome because of such issues as channel cannibalization and scarce-product management. These problems can be overcome, however, through (1) metric-driven executive behavior and compensation and (2) process discipline and open communication among the executives.

The more involved approach of the joint operation option provides the optimized allocation numbers. In addition, it tends to be easy to implement and maintain as business executives and conditions evolve.

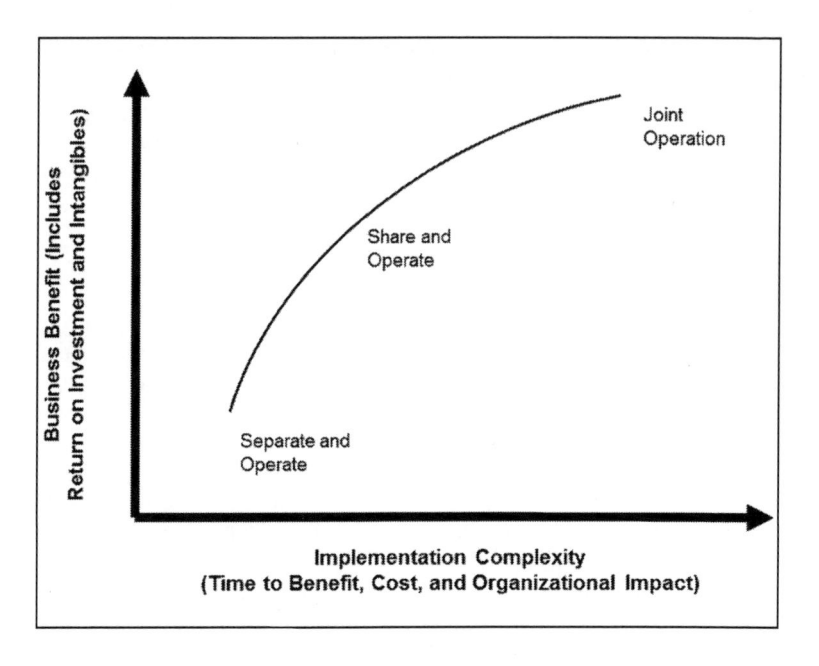

Exhibit 2: Business Benefit vs. Implementation Complexity

There are other differences among the options as well. As shown in Exhibit 2, companies experience a huge gain in incremental business benefit as they move from the separate and operate to the share and operate model. But implementation complexity increases as well and as a company approaches the joint operation model, it really starts to become a factor. This implies that after a certain amount of joint leverage, the incremental benefit may not justify the improvements in business benefit. The trick is to define your most advantageous position on the complexity curve. To move to a true joint operation, organizations will need to demonstrate total flexibility and adaptiveness.

Exhibit 3 demonstrates the huge gains in asset leverage that an organization can achieve as it moves along the spectrum of options. Assets are defined not only in physical terms but also in terms of intellectual property and vendor relationships that have been developed over time. The key in implementing any of the options presented here is to enable an organization to choose its position on both cures and communicate the value to its shareholders and other interested parties effectively. This goes a long way to dispel any perception of confusion that may arise in the financial community or among trading partners.

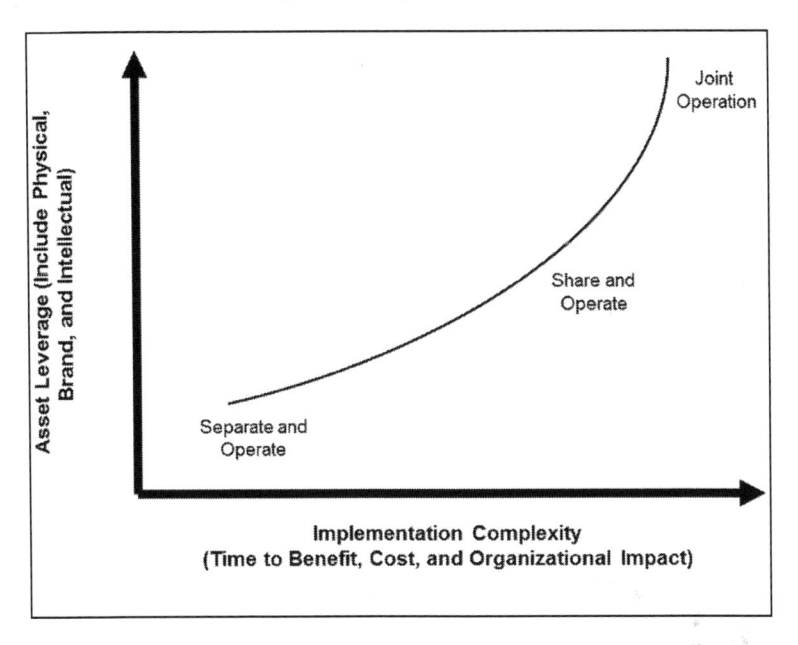

Exhibit 3: Asset Leverage vs. Implementation Complexity

There is no single option that best defines a solution for any given company. The separate and operate option, for instance, tends to work well for companies that are setting up joint ventures with other partners to enter foreign markets or new market segments. The share and operate and joint operation options work better when the existing supply chain infrastructure can be leveraged across both the physical and online businesses.

The benefits of choosing and implementing the correct model can include fixed and working capital savings that range from factors of one to three over existing levels. We also have found that customer satisfaction in the form of enhanced service and better user experience leads to higher retention levels. These advance from 10 percent to 30 percent as you move from the separate and operate option to joint operation.

e-Commerce and e-markets are fundamentally changing the landscape of businesses. The established bricks-and-mortar brands are fighting back and converting themselves into click and/or walk corporations. In the mad rush to gain ground, many are ignoring some fundamental business concepts. These shortcomings will eventually catch up to them and have a significant (and negative) impact on the overall shareholder value. We need to continue emphasizing that business fundamentals are not going away with the advent of the Internet, but that they need to be adapted to the new connected and digital economy.

Our work demonstrates that only those corporations that adhere to strong fundamentals in finance, delivery chain planning and operations, integrated sourcing, and brand leverage will survive the onslaught of the Internet upstarts and continue to demonstrate healthy growth in market capitalization. These will emerge as the click and/or walk winners.

NOTES FROM CHAPTER

UNSHACKLED PART VII

B2B Exchanges – Non Traditional Co - Opetition

Is business-to-business (B2B) e-commerce a revolution or on evolution? At this point, there doesn't appear to be a clear-cut answer. For some time now, established companies such as Dell Computer and Cisco Systems have been using the Internet and associated technology to streamline their business processes while creating a differentiated business model. Yet their initiatives involved only those suppliers and customers with which they did business. Neither of these companies can lay claim to starting a widespread revolution

If anyone could take credit for setting a revolution in motion, it would be the early independent markets that were formed in such specialized sectors as chemical / traditional MRO (maintenance, repair, and operations) purchasing. Yet despite all the hype surrounding these e-markets, none has yet delivered on the value promised to investors early on.

Exchange activity has been characterized by limited transactions, poor supplier connectivity, and lack of any real progress in disintermediating the supply chain.

With regard to disintermediation-the elimination or streamlining of links in the supply chain to foster sustained economic growth-the promise of the Internet has hardly been realized. Instead of using this powerful new technology to reduce the inherent complexity of the supply chain's physical structures, we have concentrated on making process improvements to existing activities. In essence, we have used the Internet to create another distribution channel without really changing the basic distribution model.

This chapter explores the reasons why the Internet in general and B2B exchanges in particular have failed to reach anything close to their true potential. It examines the core components that need to be a part of any successful e-marketplace.

The article then presents the rules for survival that, if followed, will provide profits for the providers and added value for the users.

The Journey to Date

In most emerging new business models, the early incumbents (like Amazon.com in business-to-consumer or B2C) tend to have the first-mover advantage. However, this does not seem to be the case with B2B exchanges, as no clear leaders have yet emerged. This does not mean that there have been no successes in this space. Rather, it means that no early enterprise has achieved dominance in either a vertical slice (an industry) or a horizontal slice (a process).

The lack of compelling success stories has been a big factor in the slow adoption of B2B exchanges over the past two years. The early exchanges used the horizontal model as a means to penetrate multiple industries at once. But they soon found that purchasing nuances in the industries they serviced (between automotive and electronics, for example) as well as the variations in supply contracts (long term fixed vs. total spot buys) made their one-size-fits-all approach inadequate as soon as it got beyond office supplies and other such commodities.

Another factor slowing, the adoption rate was the economic model upon which most of the early B2B hubs were built. It is generally accepted that the processing costs in many industries range from $40 to $250 per transaction. The main business justification used for the exchanges was the cash flow that could be generated by lowering these costs by a factor of "X." The higher the "X," the higher the perceived liquidity that was generated by the hub.

A couple of cracks in this justification model became evident almost as soon as the hubs started doing business. For one thing, companies had difficulty determining how much of their savings was attributable directly to the exchange and how much was the result of productivity increases recorded during the course of normal business operations. Further, these savings tended to have a short sustainable life. Finally, the sharing of the economic gains among the participants and the exchange became an issue. Unhappy with how the savings were being apportioned, some buyers and sellers went around the exchange and formed their own relationships.

Another problem plaguing the early hubs related to time to positive cash flow, which was typically in excess of 30 months from date of inception. Because of the market correction that occurred in the first quarter of 2009, many of these efforts and hubs were forced to demonstrate much shorter time to liquidity and positive cash flow. In many instances, this hastened their demise.

Yet another problem was the heavy cataloging that took place during the early days of the exchanges. Companies like Ariba were touting the' extensive supplier community represented in the catalogs. Participants could benefit from these exchanges as long as their focus was on purchasing the "O" from MRO. But the static, nature of the catalogs was not suited to complex multi-attribute dynamic buy, nor could these exchanges bridge the gap into the non-commodity, direct material sourcing world of long-term contracts.

Yet when all is said and done, the explicit value propositions in streamlining and leveraging the product development, purchasing, inventory management, logistics, and customer service activities by combining the power of multiple corporations across and within industries is huge, The total inventory in the system in the United States alone amounts to more than $1.1 trillion. Using a conservative estimate of savings of 5 to 10 percent in working capital improvements through B2B exchanges, we can calculate the bottom line impact at $55 billion to $110 billion. This does not include the other value-enhancing activities of shortening new product development times, enhancing customer service through greater product and information availability, and increasing workforce productivity.

The next section presents the new rules that public and private exchanges must follow to survive and prosper in an ever-changing market, and because the market is so dynamic, other factors are sure to arise that will further change the landscape. But one thing is sure: B2B is here to stay and will be the major mode of commerce for the foreseeable future.

The Survival Game

Several recent developments have emerged that will force the existing public and private marketplaces to rethink their business models and market-penetration strategies. These developments can be grouped into the following four categories: business framework, pricing framework, connected commerce evolution, and area of focus.

- *Business framework.* B2B marketplaces have often suffered from following the same misguided philosophy of the B2Cs-that is, "build it and they will come." This line of thinking implied that very little effort or thought had to go into the operational aspects of the exchange, such as logistics and fulfillment, customer service, supplier and customer integration, and channel alliances. Establishing an online presence was considered paramount; other issues dealing with fulfillment and customer satisfaction could wait. The business framework presented below considers *all* aspect of an ongoing and successful B2B venture.
- *Pricing framework.* How often have we heard that the marketplace will create its own liquidity by eliminating thousands of dollars in ongoing transaction processing cost? We've also hears over and over again that advertising and margin keep would be a major revenue source for online ventures. Although these potential revenue sources may be good starting points, they should not be the end game for any liquidity model. Our framework considers different revenue aspects like collaboration, subscription, and membership as well as transaction fees based on volume usage.

- *Connected commerce evolution.* Catalog-ware, auctioning capability, and basic content management features all were considered to be part of a successful B2B launch. Now the keys to success are found in dynamic commerce, supplier enablement, and collaborative frameworks for real-time synchronization across the supply chain, and online tracing of the order-to-cash process.
- *Refined areas of focus.* Different versions of vertical vs. horizontal and private vs. public marketplaces have been tried. In general, it seems that horizontal marketplaces with little or no sponsorship from any tenants have had the most difficult time. That does not mean that vertical marketplaces have won the war and the game is over. In fact, we believe that horizontal niche players will be among the winners going forward. The real message is to have a razor-sharp whatever model you pursue.

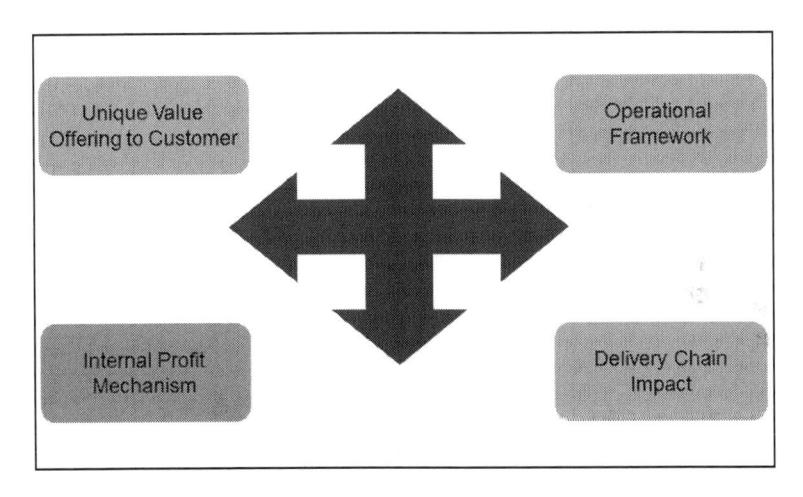

Exhibit 1: Four Components of the B2B Framework

SETTING THE BUSINESS FRAMEWORK

Our business framework incorporates four essential components for continued growth for any B2B hub. These center on the uniqueness of the entire offering for the user, an operational framework that acts as an enabler to generate rapid liquidity for the marketplace, internal profit/cash generation mechanisms that allow for sustained economic value, and a positive impact on the delivery chain. Exhibit 1 depicts these four components of the framework. For the marketplace to succeed, the four components have to work in harmony and value-added independent entities.

The *uniqueness of the offering* to the customer can no longer revolve around the depth of the products and catalog items offered. This conventional "strength in items" emphasis has led to the rapid consolidation and ultimate demise of many an exchange. Some marketplaces boast that they have access to X million SKUs and Y thousands of suppliers as their central value proposition. Though this is important, more important is the shift that needs to occur from products to services and, in many cases to a bundling of products and services.

The unique offering to the end consumer or business lies not In the availability of products online but rather in the content, service capability, complementary alliances (logistics, financing, order processing, and so forth), and total package of offerings.

Further, these services can be provided to streamline and enable rapid adoption of the buying or sharing process.

There has been a blurring of products, services, and alliance offerings in the e-marketplaces. How well the hubs can deliver the total package will be the continued differentiator for market success. In fact, we may get to a point where their product margins will be close to zero. The service and alliance revenue streams instead will be the means to rapid liquidity.

The *operational framework* and the pricing mechanics can often Determine the success or failure of any B2B offering. The operational aspect deals with how the specific product/ service or the bundle of products/ services is offered to the customer. This is a complex mix of the right scalable technology platform, the right people to give the human "touch and feel," and the right delivery of the products and services. Companies often have focused on one or two of these components while ignoring the others.

Anchored by the technology vendors, which had an equity ownership, these exchanges offered a robust technology platform. Yet they were weak on the other key components and lacked a solid business model. In any type of exchange, sound business principal must take priority over the technology platform. We only need to look at the successful hubs created by Cisco Systems and Dell Computers to understand this.

The *internal profit mechanism,* discussed in more detail later, is the vehicle through which the exchange gains liquidity from the services and products offered to its constituents. Although pricing schemes are a subject for a separate article, we need to emphasize up front that time to liquidity or positive cash flow is critical to success. The time frame has ranged from 40 months to as little as 12 months from inception. The current volatility of the capital markets will not allow for any expansion of this time frame. In fact, even more aggressive time lines could be in the offing.

Finally, the framework's *delivery chain impact* component may be somewhat controversial. We contend that for a many-to-many hub to retain sustained shareholder value, it must either significantly improve overall delivery chain performance or significantly shorten the chain-that is, disintermediate. To date, most hubs have yet to modify their chains in these ways and instead only serve as infomediaries between various trading partners in the chain. Though the short-term value of streamlined information flow is huge, we question the long-term viability of public hubs that do not change the topography of their industry. Over time, the larger trading partners will leave these hubs to set up their own private exchange relationships in the quest for greater value add.

New Pricing Framework

The debate over how exchanges should handle pricing continues with no end in sight. Going forward, though, one thing is certain:

The pure transaction-fee-based model will no longer suffice. Pricing is a complex mechanism that should be viewed along different dimensions-including type of service, life-cycle maturity of marketplace, and type of revenue source.

Essentially, B2B exchanges provide these five types of service:

- *Commerce,* which is the process of buying and selling.
- *Connectivity* services, which are a bundle of preconfigured system-to-system connections as well as service offerings to maintain the interfaces and interactions.
- *Collaboration,* a bundle of services and technology to enable marketplace-centric inventory and logistics management, production and order planning, and execution.
- *Content* services, which deliver and maintain information and search capabilities.
- *Community,* which allows marketplace participants to cross-sell and cross-merchandise to create new bundles of offerings and attract new business. The three phases across the top of the graphic that follows - initiate, penetrate, and mainstream - show the degree and speed of adoption in the marketplace being served by the B2B exchange. These two factors will determine the time to liquidity for any new marketplace entity.

Although commerce services initially (see Exhibit 2) drove the markets, collaboration services and connectivity solutions are now the main drivers. These latter marketplace offerings will provide hugely incremental value to the day-to-day operations of companies. Importantly, they will also create barriers to entry for competitors. The future of competing marketplaces will be decided by how well they differentiate their collaborative and connectivity offerings.

Marketplace's Ability to Sustain Revenue Stream Over Life Cycle			
	Initiate	Penetrate	Mainstream
Commerce	M	L	L
Connectivity	L	M	M/H
Collaboration	L	M	H
Content	L	L	M
Community	L	M	M

L= Low, M= Medium, H= High

Exhibit 2: Marketplace's Ability to Sustain Revenue

The final pricing dimension deals with the type of revenue source - that is, transaction fee, membership/subscription fee, or a combination of the two. There is no one-size-fits-all approach that applies across horizontal processes or vertical industries. Determining the right pricing approach requires careful evaluation on the part of each individual exchange. However, certain revenue approaches seem to work best for certain types of services. Exhibit 2 shown below depicts the types of revenue models now in place in the more successful exchanges.

Types of Revenue	Transaction-based	Membership/Subscription Based	Combination
Commerce		———	
Connectivity		———————	
Collaboration			———————
Content		———————	
Community		———	

Exhibit 3: Type of Revenue, Transaction, Membership, Combo

It's clear from the graphic that the revenue trend is away from purely transaction-based services. Marketplaces need to focus on helping their clients determine the exact mix of membership/subscription and transaction-based services that will be acceptable to the entire community.

The Evolution of Connected Commerce

Gone are the days of standalone commerce that is hub-centric or anchor-centric. We're now in a connected economy in which we need to enable and leverage our strategic relationships with customers and suppliers alike. Though price competitiveness will always be important, it will not be the only deciding factor in future buying decisions. This opens the door to connected or dynamic commerce. As B2B marketplaces begin to deal with direct materials or non-commodity materials and services, factors such as quality, financial stability, logistics capabilities, and ability to meet adaptive specifications will become increasingly important.

The ability of marketplaces to provide participants with access to multiattribute-based request-for-proposal (RFP) and request-for-quotation (RFQ) processes, coupled with the ability to evaluate all bids on multiple dimensions in near real time, will be a critical success factor. The first generation of e-markets were all internally focused - the "get your house in order and they will come" mentality. For markets to become mainstream, however, three ingredients must be in place: content, supplier and customer enablement, and a robust and delightful user experience.

- Content management has become an extremely important criterion for any marketplace, the ability to comprehensively search for existing content, easily add and cleanse that content, and allow for distributed content management has become an essential core capability.
- Supplier and customer enablement implies dual propagation of information and data in near real time both upstream and downstream. This capability requires connectors that are bi-directional into various enterprise backbone systems, thereby allowing for more streamlined processing and creating barriers to entry for other e-hubs.
- The concept of a delightful user experience has been extremely important in the B2C world. However, the early B2B markets ignored this principle. The basic shells used in the construction of their technical platforms allowed the hubs to be functional within months of launch. However, this approach failed to take into consideration the user's need for a productive and easy buying experience. Many of the current hubs now are focusing on rebuilding their Web sites to incorporate the same design principles found in the B2C sector. Finally, the next generation hubs will have features that enable networked value chains to collaborate effectively on product design, forecasting and replenishment, and real-time fulfillment.

Refining the Area of Focus

The B2B exchanges' area of focus has been a subject of considerable debate for some time now. Our intention here is not to provide a hard-and-fast rule on focus area but to offer some points that highlight some salient features for those hubs that have just been launched or are on the drawing boards. On the one hand, we don't see a need for many more independent horizontal hubs that provide broad-brush procurement or logistics capabilities. However, there is a real need for niche players with narrow focus areas that provide targeted high value-added functionality.

Other niche areas include multiattribute trading and bidding optimization, and revenue- and profit-based portfolio management for introducing and phasing out products and services. We believe that private hubs that are sole anchored or anchored by select members will be prevalent over the next couple of years. These hubs will allow companies to realize the networked benefit of extending their internal supply chain to suppliers and customers.

No Need to Wait

So what do the next few years look like for the B2B exchanges and their users? The answer is a complex one. But some important trends that we see emerging include the following: the advent of niche-focused and specialized e-hubs, a rapid rise of private markets, mainstream adoption of multi-company e-processes , an increased focus on generating liquidity, the emergence of connected commerce and dynamic trading, and, finally, a far more user-friendly B2B experience.

The exchange players will need to focus on value-added services as part of their portfolio. They will also have to provide end-to-end solutions as opposed to pure catalog plays. Their revenue streams need revision and refocus, too.

Does all of this mean that potential users need to wait before participating in an exchange? The answer is a resounding no. They can derive important benefits from exchanges here and now. But before entering into a long-term agreement, they need to make sure that the pricing strategy and service offerings will not change. When negotiating an agreement with a B2B exchange, for example, procurement users need to carefully consider their commodity sourcing strategies as well as the associated spend leverage being provided to the hub. They also must determine how participation in the exchange could affect their supplier relationships.

Though there is no single winning strategy for the new B2B entrants, they certainly will need to focus intensely on selecting the right revenue stream and bundling products and services in a way that completely satisfies customers. With this focus, coupled with sound technology and a proven ability to streamline the supply chain, a B2B exchange will have a fighting chance.

NOTES FROM CHAPTER

UNSHACKLED PART VIII

Optimize Supply Chains and Avoid Data Explosion

Supply chain management is the process of effectively managing the flow of materials and finished goods from vendors to customers using manufacturing facilities and warehouses as potential intermediate stops. This activity, however, isn't a new concept. In recent years, organizations have noticed that effectively streamlining the supply chain can improve their customer service levels dramatically, reduce excess inventory in the system, and cut excess costs from the network of the organization.

With the advent of Enterprise Resource Planning (ERP) vendors in the marketplace, the concept of centralized data has become a reality. As a result, new vistas for supply chain vendors have spread to provide intelligent decision making and planning capabilities for users of these systems. The future of supply chain management has become intimately tied to the emerging ERP wave that has captured the attention of corporations around the globe.

Since the late 1980s, many organizations have gone through, or are currently going through, the job of reengineering their business processes. In many instances, this effort has involved revisiting their supply chain. One Efficient Consumer Response study, sponsored by the Food Marketing Institute, estimated that 42 days could be removed from the typical grocery supply chain, freeing up $30 billion in current costs, and reducing inventory by 41 percent. Many other industries have lengthy product flows that translate into excessive supply chain costs. For example, a typical chemical industry product may go through multiple production facilities before being shipped to a customer via barge or rail car. All these components lengthen total supply chain time.

The old adage "time is money" is exemplified by the findings of a study by A.T. Kearney, a management consulting firm. The organization estimated that supply chain costs represent more than 80 percent of the cost structure in a typical manufacturing company. For retailers, it represents 70 to 80 percent. These numbers indicate that even slight improvements in the process eventually can translate into millions of dollars on the bottom line.

Improving the supply chain

We all understand the importance of improving our supply chain, but very few people have accurately defined the critical success Drivers needed to achieve improvements suggests that success depends on the several primary drivers, including the following:

- Well-defined processes with well-defined guidelines for decision making;
- Removal of organizational and functional barriers;
- Early visibility to changes in demand all along the supply chain;
- A single set of plans that drives the supply chain operations and integrates information across the supply chain.

While the first driver in this list is a given in most organizations, the importance in the remaining drivers s very high. Organizations that promote the formations of "functional silos" are less likely to achieve coordination within the various components of the supply chain than organizations that work without functional barriers. This also necessitates the integration of data across the enterprise so that common information is shared by all planners in the supply chain.

The task of improving the supply chain can be extremely complex and difficult. Various decisions integral to making improvements are forecasting, purchasing, production, storage and distribution. Forecasting initiates the entire process of supply chain management in all environments of Assemble to Order (ATO), Make to Stock (MTS) and Make to Order (MTO) One needs to know how much to make and what to make before any of the other decisions can be triggered. A good system will offer modules tailored to the decision being made, and will provide end-to-end solution starting with forecasting, planning, and scheduling, and ending up with transportation planning.

It's important for organizations to have horizontal and vertical visibility into their supply chains. Every decision involved in purchasing, producing, storing, and distributing goods are interlinked. A change in any one dimension initiates a trickledown effect on the remaining components in the supply chain. For example, planning for upcoming seasonal builds impact production, distribution, and materials. Matching a competitor's 20 percent price cut impacts the entire supply chain of an organization. If a single production line in a facility is down for a day, production must be rescheduled or moved across the enterprise to avoid delays in meeting customer demands, etc. As a result, good supply chain management systems need to be able to reconcile changes both horizontally and vertically in a computationally efficient manner.

The challenge of supply chain management is to constrain plans with multiple constraints such as materials, capacity, (production and distribution), time and locations, transportation, holding capacity, line and product sequencing, lot sizing of production quantities, production changeovers and down times, ramp up curves when switching between schedules or machines, campaign planning, multi-staging of production and distribution, and bills of materials.

The end result of all these constraints is "combinatorial explosion." Suppose there's a simple problem of planning 1,000 SKUs for an organization that has 10 suppliers, 10 plants and 10 distribution centers (DC). Assume that the network is a complete graph and the planning horizon is 12 time periods.

For this problem to be solved simultaneously, you will need 12 million place holders for each combination of SKU, supplier, plant, and DC. Furthermore, this large number grows exponentially with the increase in any of the facets of decision making. In today's environment, most organizations are increasing their SKU counts rapidly. In addition to the ever-increasing supplier base, this explosion in SKU counts renders the simultaneous decision-making process at the SKU level virtually impossible.

Generally, constraints can be categorized under three groups: material-related constraints, production-related constraints, and distribution-related constraints. In the past, software companies have specialized in materials (MRP vendors)·capacity (finite-capacity schedulers), and some have crossed into both material and capacity but with limitations on volumes or locations. In an age of rapid improvements in computing technology and better solution methodology, however, it's possible to take a broader perspective of the entire supply chain, and solve for very large SKU counts - provided you don't try to solve the entire business problem as one computational problem. The trick is to solve the business problem and, yet, avoid the black hole of "combinatorial explosion."

Options

There are four options available to combat the "explosion" effectively. They include the following:

Throw up your hands in despair and do nothing. This is the easiest option, but will result in the continued escalation of supply chain costs.

Use the coin toss principle. Some organizations use this principle to make every decision arbitrarily. This process obviates the need for any planning or scheduling software, but can be detrimental to the well being of the organization.

Boil the ocean. Some supply chain solutions are built by aggregating detail-oriented solutions from the manufacturing realm. This implies solving for every decision at all times. Every time there is a change in anyone data point in the system, one needs to resolve for the entire problem.

OPTIMIZE SUPPLY CHAINS AND AVOID DATA EXPLOSION

This reasoning makes little sense from the perspective of the decision-making cycles that exist in all businesses. While this process will lead to generating optimal solutions at all times, there are still some problems. You will need more economical, faster computers; otherwise you will be memory-bound, and you won't be able to generate rapidly entire supply chain solutions that can scale large volumes in real-time.

Decision scope based planning. The supply chain problem is mainly a "calendaring" game, intimately tied to the time-phased nature of decision-making cycles in the business world. Be sure to examine the scope of the decision being made, as well as the authority of the decision maker.

This means solving the problem by providing tools to support various levels of decision making, namely those that are strategic, tactical, and operational in nature. Since decisions made at each of these levels differ significantly, the solution procedures embedded in these tools vary. These tools also should be configured so that they are fully integrated, which will reduce implementation costs as well as time-to-benefit.

THE SYSTEM MUST MEET THE NEED

We live in a dynamic environment. Prices change, machines break down; trucks fail to show up at agreed upon destinations, customers generates sudden orders, and on and on. But we still plan even under uncertainty. This doesn't imply that planning is futile, but that care should be taken to make the right decisions at the right time. For example, don't commit a priority order that is three months .out since the demand profile may change significantly over the next few planning periods. This order commitment process shouldn't be within the scope of a strategic toot but should be used as a guideline for other supply chain decisions, such as resource planning. A decision to invest in a new piece of machinery, however, needs to be made with a time horizon that is even longer due to the lead time for delivery. This can even be accomplished by using historical data or incomplete information.

A MULTI-LEVEL APPROACH

Therefore, we can conclude that in order to build an effective supply chain management system that solves the entire business problem, scales for volumes, and doesn't require high maintenance, a company needs to adopt a multi-level planning approach.

An example of a multi-level approach would be a three-level planner. At each level, a series of decisions are made based on the decision's scope and the associated timeline. That information passed on to the subsequent levels. The levels can be tied together at the data level, at the algorithm level, or it can be a hybrid of both.

Listed below are the decision levels that might be found in an example of a three-level planner:

- *Level-One Decisions.* These decisions are in the area of business planning, and they have a long-term effect on the supply chain. Very often, detailed information is not available or reliable. Senior management is frequently the decision maker and user of this information. Quick response is not a requirement at this level since these decisions are not made or revisited every day. Examples of Level One decisions are dynamic sourcing, capacity planning, and pre build planning.
- *Level Two Decisions.* These decisions are in the area of tactical planning, and they have a shorter life than Level One decisions. Detailed. information is available, and the data probably is very reliable. These decisions are constrained by Level One decisions with some leeway to account for sudden changes in data. At this level, quick response is nice to have, and occasionally is something you must have.

An example of a Level Two decision is one that needs to commit priority orders and obey commitments made in Level One.

- *Level Three Decisions.* These decisions are in the area of operational planning and scheduling. The effect of these decisions reverberates throughout the next couple of days or shifts, and they are constrained by Level One and Level Two decisions. Quick response is an absolute necessity, and the concepts of Available to Promise (ATP) and Capable to Promise (CTP) need to be designed to work upstream with the other levels. Examples of Level Three Decisions are prevalent in the area of line scheduling, material and inventory allocation, and transportation planning.

This three-level approach emphasizes the fact that supply chain management is a series of business decisions characterized by distinct business models, which are largely influenced by location topology, product granularity, and elapsed cycle time.

The challenge in building a layered system is to avoid the problem of the "deadly embrace," which occurs when a decision made at a higher level is completely redone at a lower level and the upstream data isn't updated. When the data isn't updated, it causes reconciliation errors both upstream and downstream. As a result, the trickle-down effect should be observed and effective loop-back mechanisms should be provided to navigate between levels. A strong loop-back mechanism also allows for complete integration of the entire suite, which reduces the number of interfaces to maintain while implementing the entire suite of supply chain tools. The fewer the number of interfaces, the easier a system will be to maintain in the long term. It will also reduce the chances of a failed batch or interactive runs.

Key factors

While designing solutions to a problem, pay attention some key factors:

The information available and its associated detail. If an organization is trying to do a long-term business plan - for example, 18 months out - it's highly possible that the forecast numbers for SKU demand would either be unavailable or extremely inaccurate. This leads us to promote an aggregate level of planning for long range decisions.

Scope and authority of decision makers. Often, the use of various modules in supply chain management software attracts different levels of users. A senior level logistics manager rarely will be the primary user of line scheduling software, and a line scheduler-in 'most cases-will not be a user of long-range planning tools. This means that the tools should be built to suit a primary audience. The level of detail displayed or used also should be modified accordingly, while keeping in mind the concept of loop-backs and the" deadly embrace."

The lasting impact of the decision. Opening and closing warehouses and manufacturing facilities are decisions that have a lasting impact on the business. As a result, these types of decisions need to be made with the entire supply chain in mind, since, ultimately, there will be a trickle-down effect of these decisions on the rest of the manufacturing components.

Response *time requires to make the decisions.* Given the inherent drawbacks in economical computing technology as well as the processing speed of existing machines, turn-around time to generate solutions becomes an important criterion in deciding the inputs and outputs in a layer. It would be unacceptable for a line scheduler to have to wait a couple of hours to generate an optimal schedule by using an complex mathematical programming formulation of the scheduling problem. It's also essential that supply chain solutions be integrated so that the task of maintaining the various interfaces is lessened. The result will allow for optimal use of the implementers time. A good solution must also provide end-to-end visibility from forecasting all the way down to transportation planning. Furthermore, it's essential to provide users with the ability to navigate through the supply chain (i.e., to go through the various levels. within and across the supply chain in real time).

Tools to support effective planning

For an extended period of time in the late 1970s.and1980s, the concept of Distribution Requirement Planning (DRP) was offered as a complete supply chain management solution. DRP provides the capability to model distribution bills, and translates time-phased demand into supply requirements. It also obeys calendaring requirements for shutdowns and closings. By itself, DRP does not solve the supply planning problem. It does, however, enhance the capabilities of the logistics network of an organization.

There is no one computation that will solve the entire planning and scheduling problem. It's not possible to scale up a detail-driven solution to extend it across the enterprise in a computationally efficient manner since the problem of planning and scheduling is inherently intractable. Therefore, different computations exist for different zones of planning.

While designing scalable algorithms for the various planning and scheduling levels, it's essential to apply a best of breed approach. This approach might be a hybrid of mathematical programming techniques, goal driven heuristics, and rules based logic. But be sure to apply the right tool at the right time, however, and keep abreast of the latest in new search methodologies being researched in artificial intelligence and optimization.

With regard to the three-level planning areas, efficient algorithms are designed by allowing for true mathematical optimality in the Level One area. In the Level Two area, feasibility for all constraints is of primary importance given the extremely dynamic nature of businesses over the shorter time horizon. Mathematical optimality can be provided, but at a cost of computational time - which most users aren't willing to give up. In the third level, certain problems are best solved by heuristic (line scheduling) approaches.

Developers of supply chain software cannot and should not be committed to providing only one solution. methodology, as this will not allow for best of breed algorithmic approaches to solving the large enterprise-wide supply chain problem.

Conclusion

The efficient solution to supply chain management problems is now recognized as an integral part of the day-today function of an organization, People have realized that growing market share is not an infinite possibility since the market itself is finite. This has turned corporate attentions toward streamlining operations in order to generate savings from a slimmer and more reactive supply chain. But there is a problem associated with enterprise-wide planning: it's large and it's growing every day with the increasing numbers of SKU's and expanding networks.

Planning is further complicated by globalization, which brings its own set of problems such as tariffs and exchange rates. The challenge for solution providers and implementers of supply chain solutions will lie in effectively leveling the business problems and providing efficient SCRs. This will be accomplished by applying best of breed solution capabilities across the various modules.

This will enable companies to avoid the problem of inconsistencies between decision levels. Concepts such as distribution planning, while not being the entire solution to supply chain management problem, still have many uses.

In the end, supply chain management is indeed a calendaring game with the various levels overlapping in their planning horizons. The trick is to keep all these levels synchronized and to solve the entire business problem by navigating through upstream and downstream information.

This article was co-authored with John Turnbull in 1996

OPTIMIZE SUPPLY CHAINS AND AVOID DATA EXPLOSION

NOTES FROM CHAPTER

UNSHACKLED PART IX

Managing the Human Aspect of the Equation

In many cases, supply chain transformations have a need for process redesign coupled with varying levels of automation. However, it is quite common to hear "Our ERP system is too rigid and inflexible"; "Our CRM software really limits the sales force"; and, of course, the ever popular, "Just give me a spreadsheet."

To hear users tell it, technology platforms are inflexible and poorly suited to the ever-changing needs of the business. Or is it possible that the issues exist with the extended user community itself, which resists change and refuses to adapt to the mounting need for automation, optimization, and data-driven real-time responsiveness?

As always, the truth lies somewhere in the middle. The correct strategy, coupled with a robust process design and a scalable technology platform, will lead to successful business transformation. But it will deliver zero value to the business if we don't have the right people with the right mix of skills and abilities assigned to the right roles, and we fail to motivate them by using appropriate reward metrics.

My hypothesis is that many transformation projects fail because managers often shortchange the level of thought and effort needed to drive change management. The key message for those of us who have to deal with increasing demands on information services and daily fluctuations in customer-service requests is to focus on the two aspects of a large transformation that often get overlooked: people and measurement.

Measurement systems and incentive structures have been debated for years, and people have spent their careers attempting to perfect a system for optimizing human cohesiveness. We suggest using a balanced-scorecard approach to optimize business change in all of our major transformations. This encompasses four key elements: strategy, human factors, process redesign, and technology enhancement. A recent example from a client was designed to simplify the European business by integrating the geography's disparate processes and systems into a single global business process for transaction support. We successfully implemented the project in seven months by adhering to the four key elements of the balanced scorecard:

- **Strategy:** The goal was to create a flexible pan-European business model as an extension of a global business model, and to allow for some adaptation to local business rules.
- **Human Factors:** We undertook a rigorous change-management program that included professional training, updated job profiles, and educational programs to teach employees new skills.
- **Process Redesign:** We revised European business processes to reflect the global supply chain and finance processes with minimal deviation.
- **Technology Enhancement:** We followed minimum requirements except where more was needed to update country-specific sales processes.

Too often, we overlook the human-factor elements of change, attempting an approach that's a cross between "take the horse to the water and it will drink" and "if the horse won't drink, get a new horse." Neither approach will work. And I'm not sure there's any one-size solution for all situations. Claims by industry analysts that only half of the supply chain projects that are planned actually deliver the business value promised have been well reported. ERPs' failures are also well documented. But if you read enough of these stories and talk to enough managers engaged in these projects and the executives who run them, a pattern begins to emerge. As with any transformation, the sweet spot lies somewhere at the intersection of people, process, and technology—and so does the sore spot. When the outcome is disappointing, the source of the failure lies here as well. Usually, the choke points that cripple us are the ones that deal with human behavior and major technology incompatibilities.

Early in any transformation effort, we always attempt to isolate the potential choke points for the company. I firmly believe, as do many of my colleagues, that process choke points and minor technology glitches can always be circumvented.

It's The People ...

Projects will encounter problems of all kinds, but the most severe issues tend to be human resource- and people-related

TYPE OF ISSUE	LOW	MEDIUM	HIGH
People-related only		X	X
Process-related only	X		
Process- and technology-related		X	X
People-, process-, and technology-related		X	X
People- and technology-related			X
People- and process-related			X
Technology-related only	X	X	
Measurement- and incentive-related			X

Figure One: Issues Matrix

In Figure One on this page, we list the reasons that many projects encounter hiccups and end unfavorably. The attempt here is to associate the severity of implementation failures with the reasons they occur. There are eight possible combinations in which some sort of failure is possible in the type of large-scale transformations needed in today's connected economy.

The underlying assumptions are that the choice of technology platform is logical and the software fits the needs of the business. These imply that there are no major issues with the technology, and only minor adjustments will be needed to align the technology with the project strategy and business process.

The key message, evident from the number of instances of high level of severity in the table, is that whenever there are significant human-factor issues, the problems that ensue tend to escalate to a level that makes them difficult to resolve.

People issues address the reluctance or inability of human resources to adapt to change and execute accordingly, and they stem from three major sources: skill-set alignment, focus, and aptitude. A related issue of critical importance involves project metrics and incentive-based motivation. I'll also describe these here.

Skill set alignment is always kind of fuzzy. It is, however, critically important to project success. We often find that large-scale transformations in operations need to be staffed by people who have a good mix of skills in the following areas:

- Analytics
- Leadership
- Adaptability to rapid changes and shifts
- Strategic or big-picture thinking
- The ability to execute in breakneck fashion

While this may appear to be a wish list reflective of the perfect-person syndrome that infects so many of us, it's actually not exhaustive. The crucial success factor lies in finding people who have the right mix of attributes and are adaptable enough to modify their behavior appropriately. People whose skill sets are skewed along any one of the axes will tend to come up short in the long run.

A common mistake is to continue investing in people who lack skills that are inherently hard to learn. This applies to analytics and adaptability in particular. Analytical thinking is extremely difficult to learn, as it requires an inherent ability that's nurtured through all the various stages of growth and education. The same applies for adaptability. People are either inherently adaptable or they're rigid in their way of thinking and performing. While this kind of behavior can be modified to a degree, it's not possible to completely retrain people who veer toward the inflexible.

Focus is a subject that's often overlooked when project plans and charters are developed. I have seen too many plans that depend on an array of part-time resources. When the allocation level for project-critical resources stands at 5 percent, the results can be comical. More than anything, such lack of focus can lead an initiative down the road to perdition. Conversely, the more successful the transformation story, the more laser-like was its execution. Though this isn't a guarantee for success, it's certainly a major criterion.

Human resource aptitude is another source of success or failure. Aptitude is a skill set that becomes decisive when there's a large number of people to challenge and motivate, and a large number of conflicts that must be resolved in the course of the change-management process. People who tend to be micromanagers or heavy-handed in their approach don't fare well at this. Those people with the necessary aptitude for success are leaders who set high standards for themselves and guide team members in their tasks, but they let self-managed teams carry the charge forward. A colleague of mine who's a sailing buff once observed that the best leaders are those "whose hands are light on the tiller but are definitely the skipper." I always offer this metaphor when asked what sorts of leadership skills are needed to achieve rapid and unquestioned success in operations transformations.

SUPPLY CHAINS UNSHACKLED

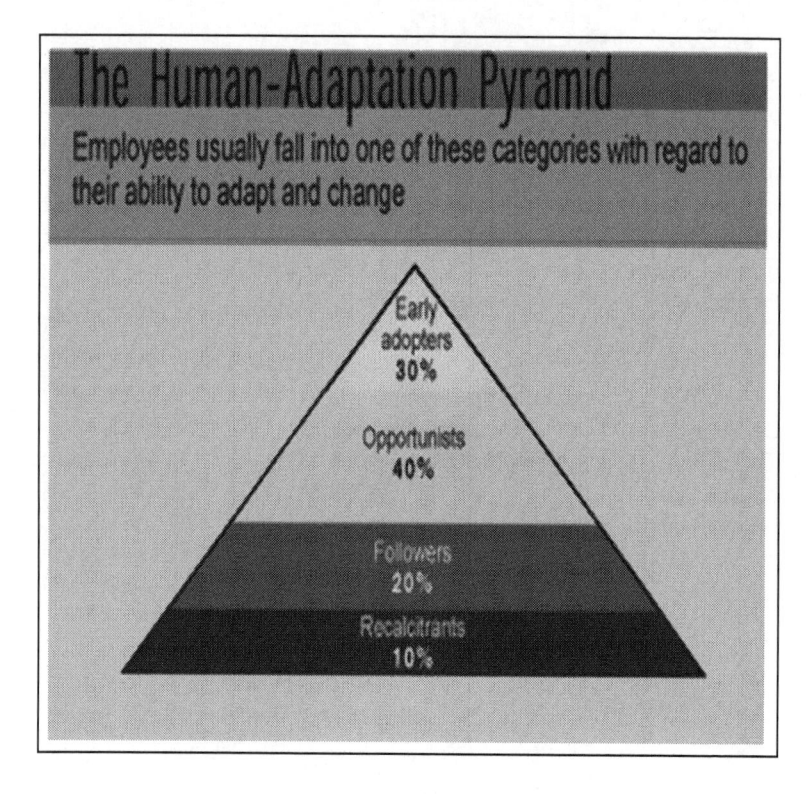

The Human-Adaptation Pyramid
Employees usually fall into one of these categories with regard to their ability to adapt and change

- Early adopters 30%
- Opportunists 40%
- Followers 20%
- Recalcitrants 10%

Figure Two: The Pyramid

Figure Two provides a practical approach to segmenting people and their inherent capacity to adapt and change. The population percentages are generalizations and not indicative of any particular initiative at any one company. The key point is that risk takers who thrive on change will be at the forefront of all major transformations—even though they make up only 30 percent of employees. More typical are opportunists—managers who jump on a successful bandwagon early in the game—and followers, who more slowly follow in the opportunists' footsteps. Change resisters are the recalcitrant's who can derail a transformation effort. Once they're identified, you may need to move them elsewhere early in the process.

Summary

Perhaps your company is planning or about to launch a major revamp of a key business process, or maybe one is already well under way. In either case, a review of the following can ensure smooth sailing for your transformational effort and give you a checklist to begin the change process.

1. Check for potential choke points

The most critical are people- or process-related, and the worst problems occur when both are involved. By anticipating potential shortcomings, you can avoid major pitfalls later.

Tally your resources. Be sure you have adequate personnel to accomplish your objectives and that the company is sufficiently focused on the project at hand. It's time to be realistic. If you lack sufficient resources at the start of a project, matters can only go from bad to worse.

2. Review skill sets

You may have enough people, but are they the right people for the job? To bring about true organizational change, you need the proper mix of analytical, strategic, and leadership skills.

3. Survey the key players

Bad attitude is a project killer, so make sure your project leaders are on board with the game plan. And don't stop there—consider your project's sponsors and clients as well. You need backers and allies who support your vision inside the corporation and among supply chain partners. Let loose the recalcitrant's.

4. Set consistent project metrics

Ensure that your key performance indicators reflect management's priorities. It's critical that your objectives and measurements are consistent for each level of the corporate hierarchy. Failing to establish consistent metrics has killed more than one program that contained all the other elements for success.

5. Personalize the project

It's one thing to tell people how they're being measured and another to explain why they should care. From senior management to junior employees, everyone affected by your project needs to understand why it matters in terms they can personally relate to.

.... And above all cascade the change at all levels of the organization

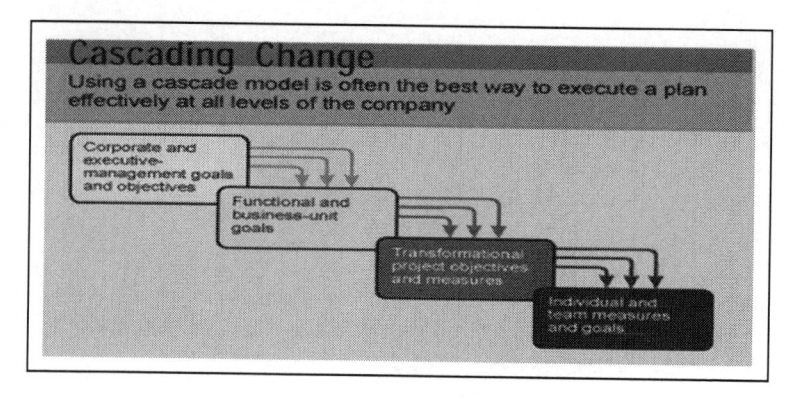

Cascading Change
Using a cascade model is often the best way to execute a plan effectively at all levels of the company

- Corporate and executive-management goals and objectives
- Functional and business-unit goals
- Transformational project objectives and measures
- Individual and team measures and goals

Figure Three: The cascade

This chapter is adapted from the authors book Virtually Vertical published in 2010

MANAGING THE HUMAN ASPECT OF THE EQUATION

NOTES FROM CHAPTER

UNSHACKLED PART X

A strategic map for Information Management for the Extended Value Community

1. Traditional information management and the role of the CIO and CTO

The intelligent use of data and information by companies is not a new occurrence. Since the early 1900's, the use of computing machines to analyze data and run their businesses has been commonplace. However, the late 1970's and early 80's, witnessed an explosion in the use of software applications to automate and streamline both front office and back office processes. We have also witnessed the phenomenon of technology being viewed as a competitive differentiator as opposed to a necessary evil for companies. This has served in elevating the position of the Chief Information Officer (CIO) to an executive position on most management committees. The rapid infiltration of technology and the constantly shifting technical landscape, has in recent years given rise to the position of a Chief Technology Officer (CTO). There are fundamental differences in the two roles and types of individuals who can be effective in either one. Later in this section, we highlight the major functional differences between the CIO and the CTO. In the field of information management, it is difficult to speak about anything being traditional. However, we have noticed that there are three types of services that seem to be fairly common across most companies. The skill sets of individuals that staff these departments are also clustered along the same lines. These are: Support Services; Information Processing and Technology Management.

Support Services: This service normally includes support for most hardware and software applications that are used to run the business. The service is typically of a technical nature and is provided 24/7 for mission critical applications. This includes all hardware and software upgrades that are provided by the OEM's as well as installation of new applications that are acquired by the company.

Information Processing: This critical service is often the backbone of the information management function in any company. In today's dynamic world, all businesses process use huge amounts of data within software applications as well as within legacy systems. The data processing function ensures that the information and data is processed in a timely manner and in the correct sequence. They also are used to balance the loads between the many hardware servers and platforms that companies use in the different functions. This service is also responsible for the various external sources of data that companies purchase from industry sources as well as the multitude of databases and data repositories that are often in use for disparate functions.

Technology Management: The technology management function is distinct from the support services but provides similar support. This service is geared towards maintaining the many applications used in the business as well as upgrades for those applications. They are also responsible for the upgrades and customized additions and modifications that may need to be performed on legacy applications as well as maintain the customized modifications for the software applications that are purchased for third parties. This function in conjunction with the information processing function comprises the business application nerve center for any information technology function.

This division in responsibilities also determines the skill sets that are found in the personnel in the information management groups in many companies. While this is adequate in environments, where information management is not a competitive weapon, it is extremely inadequate for an EVC. The main deficiencies are found, not in the capable people, but in the focus of the information management function. The traditional function is inwardly focused i.e. they view themselves as being in a support mode as opposed to a proactive and consultative mode. They tend to follow the business as opposed to be a part of key decision points in the business. They are also used to a silo mentality, when dealing with functional leaders from the business as opposed to an open and collaborative model. Finally, the traditional function focuses on retaining individuals who are technocrats as opposed to individuals who are much more ingrained in the day- to-day operations of the business.

An EVC model for Information Management

The key characteristics of services for an EVC model will include: proactive monitoring services; business collaboration services; application centric knowledge and infrastructure specific domain expertise.

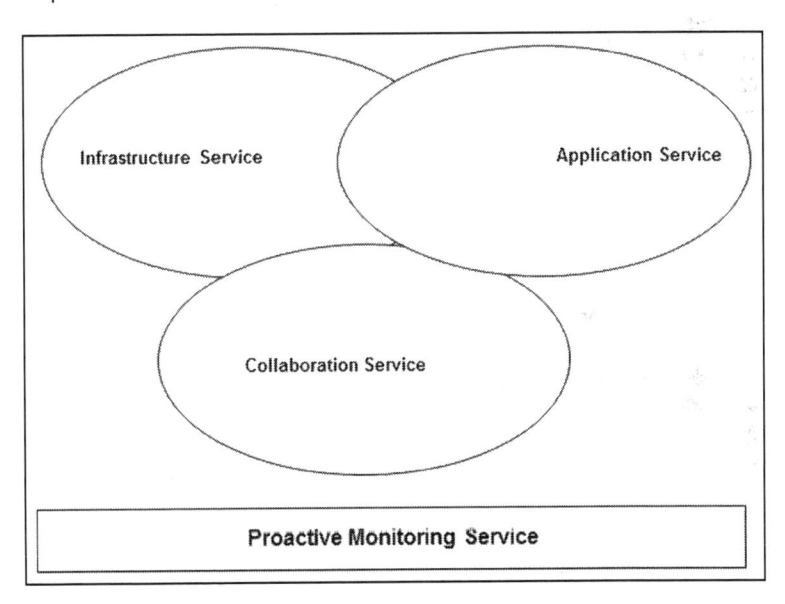

Figure One: EVC Information Management Model

Infrastructure Service is comprised of all technical hardware related services. Examples of this would include installation and maintenance of telecommunication, networking and computer (personal and business) equipment; creating and executing a secure, global deployment platform for strategic applications across all participants; creation and execution of corporate intra and extra nets; maintenance of all server farms and data centers that are operated by the company; monitoring of all outsourced partners that have an impact on hardware and response times for the business, etc.

Application Service is comprised primarily of maintaining, upgrading and customizing the various business applications that are used to run all horizontal processes in an EVC. This would also include first line support for all 24/7 mission critical applications as well as 8/5 support for all other applications. This service would also include application expertise for all legacy and third party software that is used in the business.

Business Collaboration Service is a group of proactive and business savvy individuals who are part of every key horizontal process that is offered in the EVC. These resources will act as the liaison between the business process owners as well as the application and infrastructure services. This group will act as internal consultants for the EVC and will be knowledgeable in all aspects of business operations. They will also be responsible for providing input into strategic shifts in the business from an external threats and competitive perspective.

Proactive Monitoring Service is for all practical purposes the governing body of the Information Management function in an EVC. This service sets the strategic technology direction for the EVC based on user input and emerging market trends. They are responsible for keeping the EVC in line with best practices across all three areas as well as conducting research into emerging application, infrastructure and hardware trends. They also serve as the representative of the EVC in technical matters for the outside world and other EVC's. This group should consist of the CIO, CTO and key business process owners from the horizontal functions.

In our experience, this model seems to work for the rapid deployment of most EVC's. The key issue that we have noticed occurs around the critical intersection point of all three services. It is extremely important to ensure that the three service areas intersect in pairs as well as together. The point of intersection of all three is the most critical. This point needs to be staffed by the most knowledgeable resources with deep expertise in all the services without being completely enamored by any one service. These resources are often the hardest to find and the toughest to retain due to their inherent expertise in the heart of an EVC. The monitoring service needs to pay close attention to all the intersection service resources and extremely close attention to those in the critical intersection point.

The roles of the CIO and the CTO

The emergence of technology as a strategic lever has opened the doors for a breed of information management professionals who are focused on market trends and standards setting, etc. as opposed to the day-to-day internal operations. The rise of a CTO is a key occurrence that traces its roots to the Silicon Valley (San Jose, CA) and the Silicon Alley (New York City, NY). A lot has been written and debated about the roles and responsibilities of the CIO and the CTO. Our intent is not to add to the literature clutter but to provide a simple framework that looks at the different types of responsibilities that the individuals may share.

Our framework defines the role and assigns a primary (P) or a secondary (S) rating to it to help define the person who would act as the key executor as opposed to an influencer.

Function \ Responsibility	CIO	CTO
Technology Strategy	S / P	P / S
Application Strategy	S / P	P / S
Evolving Needs for People and Process	S / P	P / S
Major project implementation	P / S	S / P
Role in promoting EVC	Inward focus	Outward Focus
Day to Day operation	P / S	S / P

Figure Two: Primary vs. Secondary Responsibility

While the above figure is self explanatory, it is important to appreciate the distinction between the two roles as well as the synergies. In general, the CTO is the external voice of the EVC as it relates to technology standards, evolution in applications that impact the business as well as needs of resources as it relates to evolving technology skill sets.

On the other hand the CIO, is much more internally focused in order to ensure the appropriate execution and implementation of the major projects within the EVC. The CIO needs to be focused on building, growing and retaining the implementation teams. The CIO on the other hand often serves as the resource that serves as the key team member for the creation of the strategies that propels the EVC's to the next level of competitive differentiation.

2. Data Centric and Application Centric view's of an EVC

A competitive EVC will need to have in its arsenal a great strategy, great people to execute that strategy and world class ability to define processes and technology to sustain and enhance the value add to the existing community and add members and value streams as the community matures. While all the categories are need to work in complete harmony, as is often the case in today's technology enabled world, the information management and implementation capabilities are differing viewpoints. We have found that the world of EVC's are lining up into one of two categories: data centric or application centric.

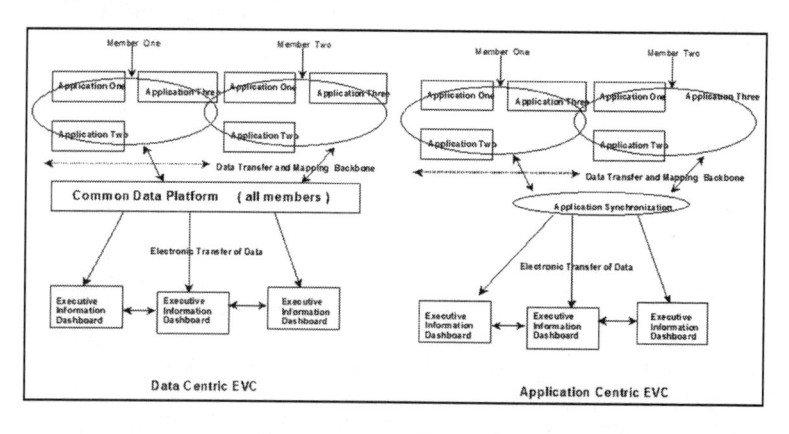

Figure Three: Data Centric View vs. Application Centric View

In Figure Three, we show the two somewhat distinct representations of an EVC's structure for information management. In the data centric view on the left, the key points are the recognition that the various members in an EVC may maintain their own sets of applications for the various horizontal processes (financials, supply chain, customer management, etc) and functions. We also note that the rapid implementation of an EVC is often determined by the ability to have a common view of data (not necessarily standard). This is accomplished by deploying a scalable and reusable data transfer / mapping backbone from providers of enterprise application integration software. The presence of the various executive dashboards is needed to allow the various member companies to conduct commerce, content and other related services between the various members and share results and information within the community. This is facilitated by deploying some form of electronic data representation mechanism like XML (Xtensible Markup Language).

The application centric view in Figure Three seems similar but has some subtle differences that can impact the method in which the EVC is deployed. The application centric view tends to assume a certain degree of commonality in the applications that are used by the members. While this is possible in many cases, it is also a barrier in many due to the presence of many comparable applications within all industry verticals and horizontal functions. The emphasis in these EVC's is often placed on gaining consensus between the majority of members, regarding the use of common application platforms. While the effort is commendable, the various intricacies and nuances of the business partners, often makes this quite Herculean. It is important in the application centric scenario, to synchronize and facilitate the exchange of data and information between companies and across disparate platforms in a many to many connection setting. The same holds true while deploying the executive dashboards.

In Figure Four, we highlight the major differences between the two distinct approaches.

Characteristics \ Approach	Data Centric	Application Centric
Ease of maintaining data integrity	Relatively easy	Difficult
Business Need driven	May be IT driven at times	Majority
Modular extensions	Relatively Easy	Can be difficult
Scalable to VC	Relatively easy	Can be difficult if on different platforms
Scalable to EVC	Relatively easy	Can be difficult if on different platforms
Degree of standardization	High	Ad Hoc
Ability to perform Peer to Peer transactions	Easy through CDP	Can be difficult if on different platforms
Executive Information sharing	Relatively Easy	Difficult if on different platforms

Figure Four: Ease of use in DC and AC

We have found the data centric approach to work extremely effectively in an EVC setting and often allows for the plug and play method i.e. allow members to join and depart, with minimal disruption to the business that is conducted by the unaffected members in any EVC.

3. The value based framework for information management and implementation

The world today is driven by value and its associated benefits for a community. The days when information management projects were undertaken with fuzzy or suspect ROI are gone for good. Companies are extremely cautious with the level of capital spending for streamlining and optimizing business processes and information technology. Many participants in activities surrounding process and technology innovation, are required by companies to put their money where their mouth is i.e. risk sharing on profits in order to ensure successful implementation of advanced concepts. In our mind, this trend will continue and the importance of execution and implementation by all members and partners in any collaborative effort will become the norm as opposed to an exception.

In any EVC, the road to implementation needs to be driven at every step by an extremely well defined ROI and rapid turnaround times for modular increments of functionality in process and technology. We believe that every modular increment should be time boxed between 2 – 4 months of effort in elapsed time. Any effort that far exceeds the guidelines needs to be carefully analyzed in order to ensure that the promised ROI is delivered.

The Information Management framework

The key tenant that we follow is to enforce the concept of " value added functions " only, i.e. no technology investments without proving that it adds value for the entire community. In order to achieve this, we use a three way classification process. The classes are: Base infrastructure (B); Significant Value add (S) and Rounding out for the community (R). These essentially mirror that fact that some of the functions are an absolute for the community to operate i.e. base infrastructure, some functions provide the key sustained revenue streams for the EVC i.e. significant value add and the others, while important for the community, is not a function that should be implemented before the EVC has had a chance to gain some momentum within its participant group. Figure Five below captures many of the key functions that are an integral part of information management in an EVC.

SUPPLY CHAINS UNSHACKLED

Function \ Category and Time Frame	Category	0 – 3 months	4 – 8 months	9 + months
1. EEB	B	X	X	
2. IT Integration	S		X	
3. Supplier, Customer and Key relationship enablement	S/R		X	X
4. Collaborative Business Planning	S/R		X	X
5. Collaborative Design	R			X
6. Collaborative Logistics	S/R		X	X
7. Collaborative Working Capital Streamlining	B/S/R	X	X	X
8. Collaborative Trade	R			X
9. Electronic Cash to Cash	S/R		X	X
10. Executive Monitoring	R			X
11. Scalable Infrastructure	R			X
12. Global Representation	S/R			X
13. Emerging Decision Analytic tools	R			X
14. Community Content Management	S/R		X	X
15. Customer Service	S		X	
16. Customer Management	R			X
17. Community Data Repository	S/R		X	X
18. Community Process Excellence Team	R			X
19. Community Technical Excellence Team	R			X
20. Community Data Integrity Function	R			X
21. Community Information Usage team	R			X

Figure Five: The Information Management Framework

EEB: In order for an EVC to conduct business independently from its participants, it is essential to get some base functions of finance and human resources operational. This will allow a community to conduct commerce and other value added transactions between themselves as well as maintain track of the usage volume between the members. The implementation of EEB is considered to be part of the base infrastructure and the complete implementation may span two phases.

IT Integration: The need to integrate many disparate systems and processes is of great importance for any EVC and its ability to sustain revenue growth. We have seen that many EVC's have underestimated the cost to create a robust integration platform that will ease the many for many connections as well as allow for processes and technology to be standardized. We see the emerging need to focus on both the technical and the service aspect of integration as a significant value add function that needs a baseline completion between 4 – 8 months in the life of an EVC.

A STRATEGIC MAP FOR INFORMATION MANAGEMENT

Key Relationship enablement: While this could be treated as part of the IT Integration service, we have found that it is distinct enough to warrant its own effort as well as timeline. As EVC's become more commonplace, the need to maintain many partnerships that are value added (like logistics, electronic payment, content factory, etc) will be essential to ensure rapid time to benefit. Similarly, many suppliers and customers may demand tighter integration and consultative services that focus on raising the level of usage in the EVC. The strategic blueprint for these services needs to be completely in place and tested with a couple of key suppliers, customers and value added providers within 4 – 9 months of the inception of an EVC.

Collaborative Business Planning: EVC's fundamentally are created to enhance the economic structure in that industry. They exist due to the inherent inefficiencies and duplications that exist in operations, sales, marketing, finance functions that are all geared towards satisfying the same end consumer or group of consumers. The need for strategic partners to plan their business together as opposed to harmonious vacuums is of great importance. Business planning will include the planning of promotions, sales campaigns, customer service and other key consumer impacted activities that provide a streamlined process geared towards the end consumer. This will improve the level of service and help sustain the importance of an EVC. The EVC must provide strategic, technical and process capabilities that allow the partners to work together but not indulge in collusion.

Collaborative Design: The need to streamline the product introduction process is an action that most industries have to deal with. This is particularly true in today's rapidly changing environment that demands short and efficiently managed product transitions. In a typical product launch, in excess of four to five partners are normally involved. This function in an EVC requires careful planning and attention as the economic value created in some industries (like High Technology and Pharmaceuticals) can range in tens of millions of dollars.

Collaborative Logistics[1]: The last mile problem has been debated during the B2C era as well as the early stages of the B2B work.

However, the issue has not been studied in its entirety. For an effective EVC, the collaboration in the logistics process between participants begins at the time that the order is placed at any node in the community. It includes all processes that are needed to fulfill, transport, promise, track and measure the customer satisfaction upon receipt of the order. It also includes the ability to dynamically price all process and capabilities based on levels of usage of the resources within the community. It is our opinion that until the logistics issue is solved along the lines of customer service and loyalty measures, EVC's will continue to sub optimize the use of the resources and hence leave behind a significant revenue stream.

Collaborative Working Capital Streamlining: This capability within an EVC deals with the strategy and process that all participants need to adhere to in order to optimize the investments in the entire EVC in working capital. As we noted in Chapter One, the willingness and the desire to streamline the working capital and the participant's ability to do so may not always be congruent. The EVC should provide strategic help, process and technology support for those members who are willing and able to effectively streamline the working capital in the community.

Collaborative Trade: In the years to come, EVC's will go global. This will be driven largely by the members global presence as well as the favorable functional capabilities that exist in other parts of the world, that can be leveraged to gain competitive capabilities across EVC's. The function that the EVC's can facilitate deals with the complex issue of international trade and logistics including transportation, customs clearing, freight and warehousing design and other related issues.

Electronic Cash to Cash: The transactions within an EVC may require the use of a third party holding and clearing house for letters of credit, cash transfers as well as proactive financing of commerce within that EVC. This service is of great importance to an EVC and needs to either be provided in house or via a third party alliance (see Chapter One).

Executive Monitoring and Scalable Infrastructure capabilities within an EVC are required to maintain sustained revenue growth within the community as well as serve as a balanced scorecard for all participants.

Global Representation: EVC's are extremely well positioned to take advantage of global trade opportunities as well as establish global partnerships that will benefit the community as a whole. However, we recommend the expansion be staged due to the complications that arise from multi language and multi currency issues. It is better to refine a business model in a location where a majority of the partners have strong presence as opposed to spreading resources too thin across all geographies from the inception.

Emerging Decision Analytic tools: All EVC's need to provide a high degree of end user customizable tools that can be used to process and use information more intelligently. The higher the degree of sophistication of information usage in an EVC, the better its chances for sustaining revenue growth in the services that are provided. However, this capability should be introduced after the basic processes in the EVC are well understood and used regularly.

Community Content Management: Dynamic content management capability is extremely important in the changing economic system that exists in every industry. The ability for all members to view, update and react to changing product specifications and new product capabilities is extremely important to maintain the near real time reactionary mode that makes the EVC powerful.

Customer Service and Management: A lot of work has been done within companies to streamline their customer service and retention processes. However, little to no work has been done to extend these capabilities to a multi enterprise environment. While the ability to provide great service is a function of supply chain, sales and the fulfillment process, customer management deals with the ability to retain, attract and provide 1:1 personalized service to your key participants. The latter capability can be phased in over time, while the former is more process oriented from the inception of the EVC.

Community Process, Technical and Data Usage Teams: As an EVC expands and matures in its capabilities and offerings, the need to provide more consultative services to all members will be a differentiating factor amongst EVC's. This will be a potential revenue stream for the EVC in the later stages as the need to optimize the processes, technology and use will be tantamount to the success of the community.

Community Data Repository and Data Integrity: The heart of any EVC will be the data that is used to make decisions by its members and participants as well as third parties. It is very important to build a base for clean data (Class A program as it relates to data management) as well as a robust platform for storing and reusing data that is needed for the members to do business. This capability is needed to standardize disparate data systems and representations in order to ensure that the EVC's response time is minimized for information updates and other related functions.

4. A Note about extensions into the key value add providers

An EVC lives and dies by the participant of suppliers, customers and third party service providers for all it's members. It becomes extremely important to device good mechanisms that encompass process management, technology implementation as well as customer management programs geared towards rewarding the providers. This is not about implementing technology that allows the system to system connectivity between the providers and other suppliers, nor is it about consultative services that allows these companies to participate in the EVC without fear of brand liquidation and it is not about the member retention capabilities that reward repeat participation and value added service. It is about all of the above in a comprehensive package that will allow the suppliers, customers and other providers in the EVC, to rapidly integrate in the EVC's that are relevant as well as exit the EVC's that are not adding value to these companies. The "plug and play" nature of these extensions need to be industry and process specific as the "one size show fits all" mentality will fail to recognize the nuances that exist between industries. World class EVC's need to device strategies that will allow varying levels of integration services based on the type of service provider and the nature of business relationship that is needed to enable the EVC to maintain it's leadership in the industry segment.

So, information management in an EVC is intertwined with the functions and capabilities that the members and participants demand. Information management is the capability that is provided to the members of the EVC that allows them to process data through the various horizontal functions and processes as well as interpret and use the derived information to make intelligent decisions in the community. Possession of information is no longer power but the use of information to make informed decisions is and will continue to set apart EVC's in the years to come.

Summary:

1. The critical intersection point between infrastructure, application and business service is the key to success in the EVC.
2. The roles of the CIO and CTO are extremely important and need to work in relative harmony to extract the best value for the EVC.
3. Proactive monitoring of the EVC performance card and constant executive interaction is a key success factor that will set apart EVC's from one another.
4. Delivered and quantified value needs to drive functional capabilities in an EVC.
5. Capabilities and functions need to be phased into an EVC based on it's level of usage and delivered benefit
6. and ... provide capabilities that allow the value added providers to interact seamlessly with all members in the EVC.

NOTES FROM CHAPTER

UNSHACKLED PART XI

Information management and the internal supply chain

1. Traditional models in planning, order management and distribution

The advent of supply chain management is not a new phenomenon. The military used concepts centered around logistics and distribution during WWII. George Dantzig, the eminent mathematician, discovered a unique method to solve large - scale linear models that represented constraints in any physical system in 1947[1]. Since, then the computing power of mainframes and midrange computers has undergone tremendous advancements and has efficiently followed Moore's Law.

However, supply chain management is not about the mathematics of the representation nor is it about large scale computing. The field is devoted to streamlining the flow of materials and information between the various groups within and across companies that are involved in the processing of information that is consumed in the process of converting raw materials into finished goods for end consumer delivery. Various frameworks have been presented over the years to distinguish the various components that comprise a supply chain. We do not intend to provide a new framework nor categorize the other frameworks that are used by practitioners. We will instead focus on the various levers of information that flows within the supply chain and is manipulated to provide intelligent decision making capability to the various functional areas like planning, order management, distribution and procurement.

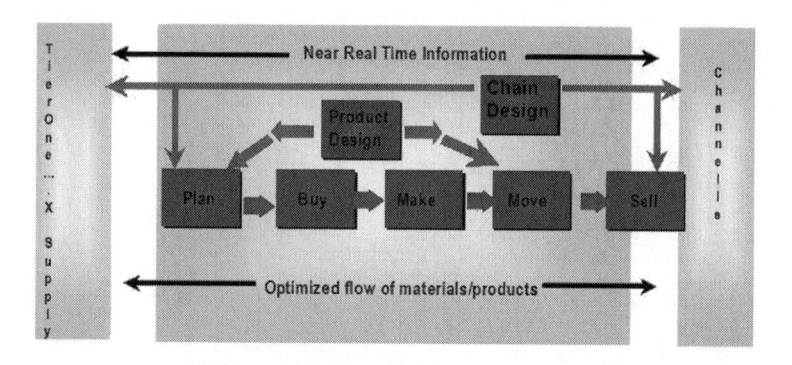

Figure One: Traditional Supply Chain Flow

The traditional model of managing the synchronization between demand and supply considers the links in the pipeline to be sequential and closely mirrors the many departmental functions that are involved in the order to delivery process. While we are not going to argue the pros and cons of this sequential and dated model, it is important to understand the basic flow of information and decisions that occur in each of the silos. The key tenets that still exist are: near real time information needs to be dynamically propagated across the silos and the channels in order to streamline the operations; and the chain should not be viewed as only internal to a company when optimizing the flow of materials and products but should be viewed as an end to end process regardless of the level of vertical integration that may exist in the company or the industry.

The process areas that make up most companies internal supply chains is shown in Figure One. We show the span of any companies supply chain or demand pipeline to extend from it's suppliers and includes it's channel partners. The process areas are design; plan; buy; make; move and sell.

Design in a supply chain includes two key components. They are new product design and supply chain design. The product design component is often treated as an engineering function that is divorced from the remainder of the supply chain. We believe that it

INFORMATION MANAGEMENT AND THE INTERNAL SUPPLY CHAIN

is an integral part of all supply chains for two primary reasons. The first being that the lifeblood of future revenue or SVM (see Chapter Seven) for any company lies in the new product innovations that are in the pipeline. Hence, this function needs to be integrated into the mainstream of the company's operations as early as possible. This will help prevent unforeseen material, capacity and other constrained resource shortages that can cause losses that exceed millions of dollars. The second reason that facilitates the need to integrate design further upstream into the decision process is the use of information that spans manufacturing, production planning and scheduling and distribution or logistics to model the total delivered cost and time focus of the new product as it migrates into the mainstream of the company's business. Data to model each silo to study feasibility as well as operational transition is resident in each of the silos and include BOM transition, capacity modeling, distribution optimization, etc. Supply Chain design is the process of creating efficient strategies that guide the behavior of a company's supply chain from the point that a product enters its domain of control to the time that the customer or end consumer has received and accepted the product. This includes design of strategies and processes in planning, manufacturing, purchasing, distribution, and order management as well as customer/consumer collaboration. Many companies think of the design process as the physical layout of it's assets and the associated product flow, but our concept of design is much broader and encompasses all the areas including the physical layout of the demand pipeline. The chain design aspect is extremely critical as it lays the foundation for the future of the companies demand pipes and collaboration pipes. It is also the main driver behind the efficient use of capital in any supply chain, which in turn drives the COGS.

The plan process encompasses the main areas of demand and supply synchronization as well as production scheduling. The key outputs from an information perspective are the demand and supply plans that are time phased and the detailed execution schedules that are a result of the plan. Other key information areas that are impacted by the process have an impact on the key interface between order management and customer due date promising as well as near real time collaboration for exception management and monitoring to the plan. For companies that operate in either a pure make to forecast or a hybrid of make to forecast and make to order, the planning process lies at the heart of the operational process that directly impacts the key working capital indicators.

The buy process area is often the most disjointed from the remainder of the processes in the supply chain. Purchasing has often been portrayed as extremely strategic but the most functionally insular in its processes and integration with the other functions. However, many companies have succeeded in breaking down those barriers to gain huge strategic benefits in hedging their risks of stockpiling components as well as other materials that comprise the bill of material. One area in which centralized procurement has allowed companies to save hundreds of millions of dollars is in the area of MRO. The major information flows that impact the work product from the purchasing group as well as allows for streamlined interaction with others are: vendor master information; product release and production schedules; production bill changes and quality level information that impacts the choice of suppliers and contracted service providers. The major information flows that impact other areas that interact with purchasing are the buying plans for direct and indirect materials as well as the strategically sourced approved vendor list based on multiple attributes that can impact the product price and quality.

The manufacturing area has probably been the best optimized from a pure supply chain perspective as the myth of optimized per piece cost implies optimized supply chain is still prevalent. While this has led to many companies losing sight of the key concept of total delivered cost, it has allowed the shop floors to operate in an optimized manner. The key information flows in and out of the factories are production plans and updated schedules as well as updated near real time work in progress and finished goods inventory levels that allow for the replenishment of the products. The future of information from the floor will hinge much more on proactive monitoring of real time capacity and capability as opposed to the static flow through data that is received after the fact. This will allow companies to migrate their pricing and inventory management mechanisms to be more aligned with total supply chain working capital efficiency goals.

The move or the logistics are has also been optimized in many companies in a silo and not as a part of a larger total delivered cost perspective that supply chains need to maintain. Companies have spent a lot of time and effort to optimize the warehousing and transportation activities that include warehouse layout, inventory management, routing and scheduling, freight management, load planning, etc. All these are value added activities that can impact the bottom line in a significant manner. However, in the larger scheme of an EVC, the component of final delivery is small when compared to the overall supply chain costs. This implies that the future of information management for the move area lies in better coordination of their activities with the other processes particularly in the areas of order tracking and tracing, near real time inventory promising, rapid flow through times at the stocking locations or cross docks, dynamic re-sourcing and deployment of products, alignment with emerging network models like hub and spoke and reverse vendor managed inventory, and dynamic and consolidated commerce for transportation and warehousing related purchases.

The sell area has often been given less importance in the traditional supply chain model that was inwardly focused as opposed to an EVC focus. The selling component should be viewed in three distinct pieces: customer and channel management and deals, customer after sales service and customer promises. While all three areas impact the supply chain, it is the first and the third that have the most impact on how any companies supply chains interact. The future of information management lies in managing multiple and conflicting channels as well as dynamic pricing in the channels based on consumer pull through. A great example of a company that has successfully priced same product differently based on the channels served is Coca Cola Enterprises. It is often a common sight to see the same bottle or can of the drink with varying prices based on the pull through. The area of customer promising holds the key to the future success of an EVC for fixed asset and working capital improvements based on varying the levels of asset utilization based on consumer pull through and desire for immediate needs fulfillment. This is also the area in which near real time information flow regarding utilization, product availability, transportation and storage capacity and capability as well as dynamic shifts in end consumer pull through will enable a seamless and as frictionless a supply chain as possible.

While the above processes and areas are the main areas for information flow management, the exercise in the migration of traditional chains into the EVC is impossible without the participation in the exchange of information that is bi – directional with the channel partners for consumption and usage rates as well as the supply base for commodity availability and the value added service providers for utilization and availability.

In Figure Two, we show a schematic of the end- to-end information flow for a traditional supply chain that demonstrates the connected nature of all the information flows and related impact on the various processes.

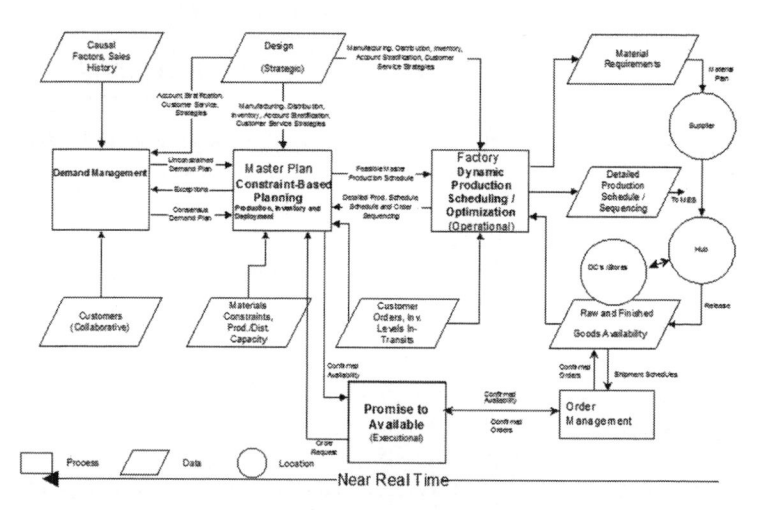

Figure Two: Information Flow in a traditional Supply chain

The major sources of information can be grouped into four major categories. They are strategic, collaborative, operational and executional. The key impact areas across the major process areas span the entire traditional silos of any internally focused supply chain.

The types of data mentioned above are segmented accordingly for a specific purpose. We have observed many companies struggle with the concept of data integrity and effective data management across the extended supply chain. Just as not all processes and functions provide the same amount of value added benefit for the organization, various types of information tends to hold varying degrees of significance.

Strategic data elements are those that would be considered sacred and crown jewels within the company. These data elements form the lifeblood of the business function that the company operates within. The data elements may be dynamic to accommodate shifting business models and strategies. Some examples of strategic data elements are customer sales history, real time pricing and promotion information, competitor market intelligence as well as dynamic capabilities of all partners in the EVC.

Collaborative data elements for an EVC comprises of the type of data that is extremely strategic to the business but is better served by jointly partnering with external sources to spread the burden of collection and maintenance. Examples of this would be the tracking and tracing information as it relates to orders, variations in competitive product pricing in the market, dynamic capabilities of partners to leverage spot opportunities for economic benefit in all aspects of the supply chain, etc. Operational data elements are those that a company would normally need to have access to in house or have plans to gain relatively easy access in order to facilitate the day-to-day operations of the business. Production schedules and plans, BOM's, lead times across and within the network, purchase orders, accounts payable and receivables, etc all fall into this category.

Tactical data elements are those that are nice to have and would improve the operations of any company but should be evaluated on a case-by-case basis to determine the cost benefit equation that would facilitate the implementation and ongoing support for the data type. Examples of this would be real time machine yield information in a consumer packaged goods environment, and dynamic personnel scheduling information in environments that are more automated than not.

The key to segmenting the data needs of any company lies in the underlying business model that is used to create shareholder wealth. While segmenting the information, it is extremely crucial that all aspects of cost (collection, maintenance, implementation as well as business sponsorship) be considered prior to embarking on the journey. We have witnessed many situations where companies implement fire drill like activities to perform one time clean up of data or one time collection of data and have no plans in place for the continuous monitoring loop that is inherently fundamental to the ongoing success.

In Figure Three, we show a classification of various data types in more detail but would like to caution the reader that there does not exist a cookie cutter solution that would fit all industries or all supply chain go to market strategies. In chapter six, we present a data classification that serves as a launch pad for the future of the customer centric supply chain.

Type of Information	Strategic	Collaborative	Operational / Tactical
Capacity		X	X
Capability	X	X	
Pricing	X		
Point Of Sale or Consumption	X	X	
Participants	X	X	
Locations	X		
Bill Of Material			X
Forecast		X	
Schedule			X
Constraints		X	X
Inventory	X	X	
Lead Times		X	X
Calendar			X

Figure Three: Classifying Data Types

It is key to note here that the various types of data and information have a cascading effect in the entire supply chain. The information processed at the higher levels of decision-making serve as a guide post for the decisions that are to be made closer to the execution of the actual order satisfaction. An example of this could be the process of dynamic sourcing of products within a supply chain. The strategic information is used to help determine the optimal locations or suppliers who should participate in the sourcing of the raw or finished good. This cascades into the collaborative demand management and master plan to enable a smaller set of alternatives to be considered for the collaborative plan that is shared with the customers and channel partners. This cascades into the executional and operational plan that is used to make and satisfy the order. In every step, the degrees of freedom in the supply chain are less that in the previous level in the information hierarchy. This does not imply that the supply chain is sub optimized in any way. It is a practical method to mange disruptions in the supply chain as well as factor in the inbuilt latency of lead times as well as physical processes that consume time and add to the order management promise date.

Figure Two is meant to serve as an illustrative example that is geared towards a more discrete manufacturing environment as opposed to a process-oriented situation. Another key factor is the presence of near real time information across all the hierarchies of information. The timing of the interactions is one that is situation specific and is dependent upon the flexibility and inherent latencies that are built into every supply chain. We have seen examples where the strategic information is revisited every quarter, collaborative is monthly and operational and executional are bi- weekly or daily. However, there is no one size fits all solution for this problem and varies within and across industries.

2. Value drivers across the traditional and emerging supply chains

The value drivers for traditional supply chain management are well understood and documented. However, we have found that there is a distinct lack of translation of the benefit streams into the value creation and core competency concepts. The traditional focus of SCM has always been on the improvements to the bottom line via an operational improvement play. Our focus is on making improvements to the operating profit margin that allows the company to focus not only on cost reduction but also on improving market share.

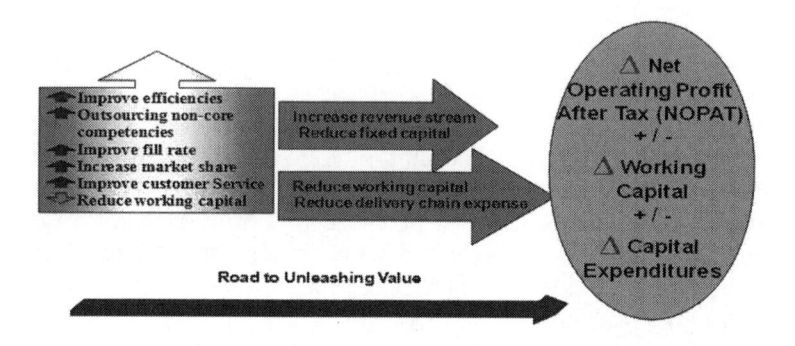

Figure Four: Value Levers for SCM

In Figure Four, we present a framework that encompasses the traditional supply chain value drivers as well as introduces the market growth and core competency framework. The traditional areas that have always been targeted for operational improvements are in working capital reduction via inventory and service level adjustments. That is also translated into improving fill rates and hence providing a large delta for working capital. Indeed, we have found that in many industries and companies, there is a potential to improve working capital positions in excess of 25 – 40% over current inventory capital tie in by improving the processes of demand and supply management as well as inventory optimization. Another common area for reduction that is targeted by traditional supply chain projects is to focus on reduction of fixed capital via rationalization of the delivery and production network. This can often uncover benefits that directly impact the amount of fixed capital that a company needs to expend to maintain its current and emerging service levels.

The new economy is primarily concerned with a focus on being world class in a set of core competencies as opposed to the more traditional vertically integrated models that were prevalent in the late 20th century. In order to facilitate this, supply chain practitioners need to focus on the revenue streams that are keeping in line with the new rules. These revenue streams and operational savings can be grouped into three areas. They are: outsourced or virtual savings; market share improvements and seamless integrated process improvements. We discuss each one in more detail keeping in mind that not all of these are relevant in all industries or verticals segments.

Outsourced or virtual savings: The days of complete soup to nuts ownership of any supply chain is over. Companies that are vertically integrated and try to make all process areas their core competencies will not succeed in the new economy. We have found that outsourcing portions of the supply chain that are not value added to companies that have a laser sharp focus on those areas generates fixed and working capital improvements in excess of 10 – 20%. This can be in the form of many types of virtual arrangements across many process areas. Figure Five below highlights some of these areas as well as arrangements that can be used to drive value creation.

Process Areas	Type of Virtuality / Arrangement
Purchasing	Centralized or GPO
Logistics	Outsourced completely or shared service
Planning	ASP model
Manufacturing	Contract
Sales and Service	Distributors or Shared model for end customer interaction

Figure Five: Types of Outsourced Arrangements

There are many types of arrangements that are being used in different verticals these days with a focus on squeezing as much out of the supply chain as possible. In purchasing, we have found that the focus on MRO as well as direct by centralizing these functions allows companies to become more competitive. The next step is to use existing group purchasing organizations or exchanges to perform these functions to further streamline the value created. Similar logic can be applied to the logistics function that would include warehousing and transportation. Contract manufacturers is not a new concept and will be used more pervasively in many industries as products become more commoditized and the differentiator lies in the brand and the marketing around it. Similarly, the end distribution can be viewed as a channel for the existing distributors or a combination of a shared process with the logistics providers. Planning has traditionally been viewed as a core function of many companies. We believe that while the process of planning is core for a company, the tools, techniques and the processes used to generate plans is not and should be viewed as a candidate for an application service provider based model. We also believe that there will be a new type of company emerging over the next five years or so and will offer entire end-to-end supply chain outsourcing services across and within industries. These companies will command significant respect of the financial markets as they will truly be the catalyst that will unleash the value of the EVC's.

Market share improvements: The traditional operational efficiency plays were not geared towards improving market share as a direct result of improving customer service. As supply chains are becoming more collaborative, we see that the advent of collaborative business planning with suppliers and customers enables an improvement in a couple of points of market share due to increased consumer and retailer confidence as well as optimized inventory management at the point of consumption. These efforts can be grouped under the CPFR[2] umbrella but is more a result of collaborating on the task of consumer fulfillment as opposed to the upfront planning that CPFR provides.

Seamless integrated process improvements: The final area for improvement in free cash flow before taxes or NOPAT, is a direct result of an integrated S&OP (sales and operations planning) process that allows all supply chain functions to proactively work on a collaborative solution for out of stock, consumer complaints, unforeseen shortages and schedule slippages. All these are root causes of decreased consumer confidence and results in reduced service levels that impacts the top and bottom line for the company.

1. Extending the one to many value chain using dynamic information

The new economy demands that the participating companies focus on the enabling the entire EVC to be better off in terms of price, quality, service and product availability. This has enabled certain collaborative business practices to emerge within and across industries as well as service partners. It has also enabled for a great deal of co-opetition amongst traditional rivals as they all focus on their core competencies as opposed to all aspects of the supply chain. We present a framework that demonstrates the new collaborative model for business management that is geared towards only end consumer satisfaction and is enabled by the intelligent use of dynamic information.

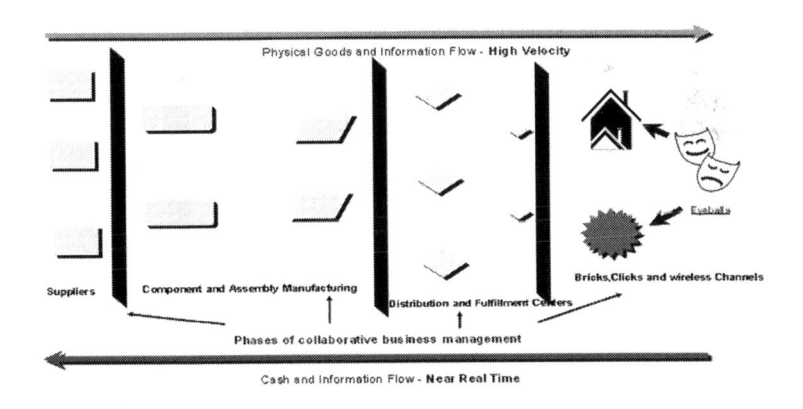

Figure Six: Networked Collaboration

The use of dynamic information from the end consumer channel that includes near real time point of purchase information; stock levels across all end consumption channels; dynamic competitor pricing from the various points of consumption as well as information from upstream the supply chain that deals with capacity and capability; and dynamic supplier product availability allows us to create a correctly latent model of the end-to-end supply chain that does not need to be viewed in silos. This dynamic information allows us to create a collaborative business management framework in which all participants have access to the same information and hence use the information to create competitive advantages for themselves as opposed guesswork based to inherent discrepancies in the sources of information that are used to measure the final goal of end consumer satisfaction and repeat purchases.

The four phases of collaborative business based on dynamic information processing are: collaborative consumer satisfaction; collaborative channel satisfaction and resolution; collaborative production and collaborative purchasing.

Collaborative consumer satisfaction:

The use of dynamic information to measure the satisfaction and purchasing of products by the end consumers across all channels (stores, www., and mobile) and the transmittal of such information with minimal latency will allow for increasing consumer satisfaction as well as dynamic pricing of products based on real time sell through. This model to dynamically price products will allow for companies to be extremely competitive and hence reduce inventories that would otherwise remain in the channels or be returned back to the OEM's.

Collaborative channel satisfaction and resolution:

The use of dynamic information on stock availability across the channels as well as the product sell through information will allow for the intelligent use of that information to satisfy all channel needs in near real time or with the right amount of latency, based on better transportation routing and loading of products. This will allow the channels to receive products that are selling in the correct regions or geographies as opposed to the static receipt of scheduled shipments based on static plans that have used outdated information as a starting point.

Collaborative production:

The use of dynamic information in the later parts of the supply chain will allow for a better schedule of production and customer promise dates that are based on realistic information of sell through and other bottle necks. Also, the use of dynamic information from within the four walls of the manufacturing and internal distribution mechanisms will allow for the schedules to be flexed based on capabilities as opposed to availability and the products to be priced based on utilization of resources as opposed to standard costs. This will allow the end consumer to receive optimal pricing for products as well as gain increasing confidence in the ability of the supply chain and the EVC to deliver on the promises.

Collaborative purchasing:

The advent of B2B hubs that we have seen before, was the first step in collaborative purchasing that the new economy experienced. However, it is just the tip of the iceberg as it relates to supply chain benefits that can be derived from the use of dynamic information. The intelligent use of information regarding sell through of the final product as well as the dynamic pricing that the market bears will need to be translated into dynamic purchasing contracts for direct or bill of material related information as well as the creation of futures markets in many commodities that impact the production of raw materials. We will also see a market for companies that can provide insurance policies against the hedges for companies that are apt to use the dynamic information to their advantage. These concepts will change the nature of the work that purchasing professionals perform and will alter the nature of contracts that are written in today's supply chains. This shift in work will be a necessary ingredient for the success of the collaborative business model in an EVC.

The new economy is forcing the supply chains to be viewed more like supply circles and supply webs as opposed to the linear parentage. This phenomenon will continue well into the 21st century and will force companies to focus more on their core competencies as opposed to the vertical models. The intelligent use of dynamic information will determine the competitive positions of the various companies. It is indeed true that supply chains will compete and not companies but it is more evident that dynamic information managers will be successful as opposed to the static managers in any supply chain. Companies should maintain a focus on their core competencies and outsource the portions or the entire supply chains as a means to remain laser focused on their markets and brands.

Summary:

1. Focus of traditional supply chain management needs to be enhanced by the addition of design and near real time information into it's framework
2. Information linkages among the supply chain processes is extremely co-dependent and should not be viewed or used in silos
3. Information for supply chain management can be categorized into four: strategic, collaborative, operational and executional
4. Supply Chain value drivers should focus not only on improvements to the bottom line of a company but also on top line growth in market share
5. Advent of supply chain outsourcing companies will provide the necessary linkage to execute on the concepts of an EVC

The previous two chapters are adapted from The New Rules by the author and published by Spiro Press in 2002

INFORMATION MANAGEMENT AND THE INTERNAL SUPPLY CHAIN

NOTES FROM THIS CHAPTER

UNSHACKLED PART XII

Utilizing Mobility to Enhance the Supply Chain

Recently, I was sitting in the audience listening to the CEO of a leading business intelligence platform provider deliver the keynote speech at his company's annual user conference. CEOs typically use the user conference as a vehicle for announcing a major launch—and this time was no different. This particular launch involved the deployment of reports and order management capabilities on the iPad. It all looked really cool and there was the obligatory audience applause. Yet as I read the material provided, it became less and less clear how the deployment would drive business value in the core or extended supply chain for users. Was the benefit derived from receiving the information on a device that you could carry at all times? Or was the value in being able to understand the information as you made another mad dash to the next customer? Maybe it was the ability to change your business processes in the supply chain to enable better execution? Or was this just an IT-driven exercise that would involve millions of dollars spent in delivering static old information on the go? Despite my lack of clarity over the promised benefits, the CEO was certainly on to something. A recent study by ARC Advisory Group of supply chain executives showed that 69 percent were using smart phones as mobile technologies in their daily operations. Twenty-two percent said they were using their phones to scan bar codes and another 22 percent said they were using the devices to take pictures of receipts at the dock. In fact, mobile devices, smart phones, iPads, "iEverythings" seem to have taken over our worlds. In the supply chain context, some of the promised benefits of mobility focus on potential reductions in freight and labor costs, better decision making via enhanced information sharing, and improved customer and consumer service levels thanks to the real-time responsiveness delivered via mobile capabilities.

Mobility essentially enables the supply chain person to do his or her job anywhere or anytime Yet we believe that not all companies will benefit from mobility in the same way. In this article, we offer an approach for determining the impact that mobility (or "M") will have on an organization. This approach is based on an analysis of business type and on the relative importance of mobility to the value chain "mega" processes— i.e., Plan, Buy, Make, Move, and Sell/Serve, which we derive from the Supply Chain Council's SCOR (Supply Chain Operations Reference) model. Readers can use the resulting framework to gauge their Mobility Index, which can be used to determine how beneficial mobility can be for their supply chain.

Four Steps to the M Calculation

We suggest the following four steps to help you derive the M index calculation that is relevant for your business:

1. Identify your business segment according to its main operating principles: Make to Stock; Build to Order; Assemble to Order; Grow to Market.

2. Determine the relative importance of the supply chain mega processes—Plan, Buy, Make, Move, Sell/ Serve—to your business.

3. Gauge the relative importance of mobility for each of these processes.

4. Derive the "M" (mobility) index for your business segment by analyzing the results of steps 2 and 3. We discuss each step in detail below.

Step I: Identify Your Business Segment

While thinking through the applicability of M to your business, you first need to examine the fundamentals of the business strategy that characterize your business/industry. Most manufacturing industries and businesses can be segmented into one (or in some cases a hybrid) of the following four segments:

- Make to Stock (MTS)—typically associated with consumer products, electronics, chemicals, health care (pharmaceuticals), automotive.
- Build to Order (BTO)—industries include construction, heavy manufacturing, aerospace and defense.
- Assemble to Order (ATO)—associated with high technology (hardware) and semi-conductor.
- Grow to Market (G2M) —agriculture is the main industry here.

Every manufacturing-oriented business tends to fall into one of the above classifications in terms of getting product to market. In some cases, individual business units within an organization may fall into different segments. The degree of responsiveness required in the extended supply chain tends to vary by business segment. For instance, the faster the time-to-market and less stock buffer, the higher is the degree of responsiveness

that can be absorbed/utilized in the business. Also, we find that the main business processes are fairly homogeneous across all segments—that is, Plan, Make, Move, etc., all tend to accomplish the same end objective. The main difference is the relative importance of each process, which is driven by the business model of the particular segment.

Steps 2: Determine Relative Importance of Mega Processes to Your Segment

Step 3: Determine Relative Importance of Mobility for Each Process

We discuss Steps 2 and 3 together because of the close linkage of the mega processes and the importance of each process to each business segment. To guide our discussion, we use the supply chain process framework shown in Exhibit 1. Identifying the relative importance of each process to your business segment and the relative importance of M to each process are the essential steps in determining your company's Mobility Index.

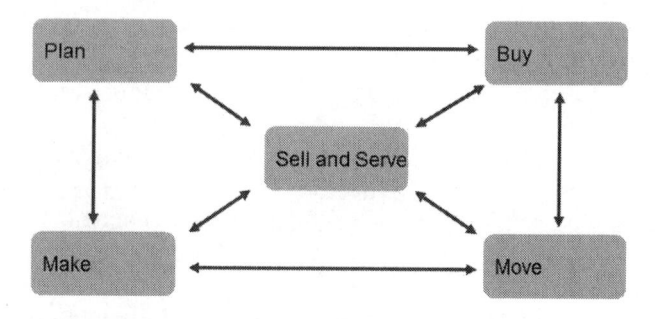

Exhibit 1: Mega Supply Chain Process

Plan: The planning function can be categorized into constructs around demand, supply, manufacturing, and distribution. This categorization of sub-processes requiring planning holds true regardless of the industry type, though the complexity will vary depending upon the business segment (MTS, BTO, and so on). We have found that in all of the segments there is an inherent process latency that is built into planning (one exception being real-time order promising). In many cases this latency varies between weekly and monthly (such as in the case of most MTS, ATO, and BTO environments). In some instances daily planning is necessary. However, the decisions made for that timeframe tend to be focused more on the rapid follow-through and execution of decisions made prior to the daily decision-making. Hence, the process latency should be used as a major indicator of the benefits that can be derived from utilizing and accessing data via mobile means. In most cases of planning, we believe that mobility usage would focus largely on accessing data across platforms and locations as opposed to using the data to drive further responsiveness in the value chain. The exception to this rule would be in the order promising constructs in which the utilization of mobility (in terms of data accessibility and portability) would make the supply chain more agile while potentially lessening the latency in the value chain for that date-promising process.

However, we should also note that data accessibility and portability will always come at an additional cost for IT infrastructure. Accordingly, the added cost should always be traded off against the purported benefit (more on that in a later section).

Buy: This function in every supply chain deals with the sub-processes involved in procuring the goods and services required for a company to perform its core business. For the purpose of this article, we can partition the function into its major processes of strategic sourcing, P2P (procure to pay) transactional support, and monitoring for compliance. Strategic sourcing is the Buy sub-process in which a company balances its spend management for key products and services so as to continually improve baseline price and performance. This is often done via vendor rationalization or a material source shifts—i.e., moving closer to the source of material especially if it is a byproduct of another. As with the planning function, we posit that utilization of the M index would center on the accessibility of data across platforms and locations as opposed to using the data to drive any further responsiveness. You can always find exceptions to the rule, of course. One that comes readily to mind is using strategic sourcing as well as other parts of the supply chain mega processes in times of disasters and supply chain disruptions. (The recent events in Japan are testimony to that.) Many corporations around the globe have optimized the sub-process of P2P transaction processing. Payment processing, for example, tends to be largely a non-strategic back office function in most companies. For this activity, using aspects of M would likely add unnecessary costs to a function that is already burdened with costs and tightly controlled.

Make: For many years now, academics and practitioners have been seeking to optimize the make (manufacturing) mega process. It is quite amusing to note that research on the job shop model with its billion variations still keeps academics up at night. I often wonder why the work on operational optimization continues to be U.S.-centric, given that most manufacturing has migrated to the Asia/Pacific region. For the purposes of understanding the M index, we focus on the following Make sub-processes: shift scheduling; labor scheduling and management; traceability; and shop floor control.

Shift scheduling continues to be crucial for the stabilization of supply chain triggers and utilizing real-time data accessibility to manage around downtimes and unforeseen outages. Mobility in this sub-process will add to the continuous improvement processes that tend to be in place in large corporations.

Labor scheduling and management within the operations center or plant is a large cost driver with enormous impact on COGS. Utilizing M constructs around data analytics to solve labor-balancing problems in real time has the potential to add economic value in operations. Additionally, many plant operations have attached warehouses in which the same labor balancing construct can be applied (oftentimes that part of the cost tends to be classified under the distribution cost).

Product /Lot traceability has gained more prominence in recent years because of the myriad recalls that have occurred in the manufacturing and agricultural sectors. Traceability that is often mandated by Federal agencies has added cost to the affected companies while driving the use of remote sensing and monitoring technology that needs multiple sites for data collection and submission. In the agricultural industry, it is commonplace to find machines being used that are enabled with mobile printing and tracking technology for tagging and labeling produce as it is harvested from the farms. This data can then be remotely sent for analysis and logging to track field packaging at the lot levels; it also can be used to perform quality assurance and productivity analysis. This capability can further support the reverse logistics processes that may be required in given industries.

Shop floor control is one sub-process that has to operate in real time or near real time. This area has been managed quite well in automated facilities that utilize PLCs and end-of-line monitoring, optimization, or simulation capabilities. There are benefits to be gained by collecting and analyzing that data in real time. Yet the cost of deploying that across the portable platform in a ubiquitous manner far outweighs the potential benefits.

Move: The process of transporting and storing the physical goods to either the end consumer or to an intermediary channel partner has become more critical as fuel prices rise, carrier capacity tightens, and imports of manufactured products increase. For our discussion purposes, the major sub-processes of this Move function that are relevant to the M index include goods routing, labor management, dock and yard management, and inventory visibility.

The sub-process of *goods routing* covers the movement within an organization's network (including within a warehouse) as well as routing to a channel partner. The real-time capabilities of mobile processes and technology could be very beneficial for routing, tracking and placements as well as for load balancing inbound and outbound hauls. These capabilities are often overlooked by manufacturing/assembly companies but are well recognized by services providers such as 3PLs.

Labor Management is a large cost driver in Move, just as it is in Make. And as in Make, mobile capabilities and analytics could be employed to further drive productivity. (Note that our analysis assumes non-union environments since unionized environments in many cases may have agreements in place that would impede the use of some of the process analytics).

Dock and Yard Management sub-processes tend to be very labor intensive and static even in today's agile supply chains. We have found that companies tend to treat these activities as necessary evils that have to be managed to get goods flowing. However, inefficiencies in dock and yard management can often be causes for customer service problems because of longer- than-necessary dwell times or even missing assets (yes, even something as big as a trailer can sometimes go missing for a few hours or even days in crowded locations). The ability to provide traffic flow based on dock schedules and yard placements can be a supply chain throughput advantage.

Inventory visibility and associated timeliness within the network is largely based on the company's supply chain operating model, lifespan of its products, and cost of the inventory. We find that real-time tracking and tracing is not a necessity in all business environments. A general rule of thumb is that the higher the value of inventory/the shorter the product lifespan, the greater the potential of mobility in improving inventory visibility. Note that there are some industries in which government mandates for product visibility dictate the business process and information needed to support the mandate.

Sell/Serve: For our discussion, the sub-processes under Sell/Serve include order transaction management; tracking, and service visibility and associated analytics.

Order transaction management can be viewed as the ability to take orders anywhere, anytime and be able to submit them for processing in the same fashion. This capability can be used quite effectively, especially in businesses that can use remote order processing to influence sales. The capability also is useful is establishing promised deliver dates or resenting customers with options (intelligent shopping) while they are browsing in their location of choice. While mobile will never supplant the traditional order receipt processes, it can effectively add a layer of customer intimacy and intelligence to a largely back-office function.

Tracking is probably the most easily understood sub-process post order entry. We are all familiar with the process of tracking a FedEx or UPS package. Automotive manufacturers, particularly in the luxury brand segment, also have developed this capability on static devices (mainly PCs), but could hugely move the needle on customer intimacy if they could accomplish the same with M. While some may debate the direct benefit of the portable process overall, most do recognize the huge value of mobility in enabling customer intimacy. This is especially important for the luxury brands that cater to a segment of buyers that have become more tech-savvy and are quite demanding in the face of competing alternatives.

The *service visibility and analytics* sub-process is an essential part of channel partner and consumer intimacy programs that alert us to potential problems before we get the dreaded customer calls. And when a problem does arise, M enables a more rapid response. This is particularly important in the B2B arena since customers tend to be large and their concern with and visibility into issues more intense. Given the non-centralized nature of the human resources and processes that typically govern our supply chains, it is important to be able to view, analyze and act on service resolution issues based on approval levels from disparate locations and by utilizing smart device capabilities (similar to issue escalation processes within IT). The processes surrounding the appropriate resolution mechanisms must be carefully designed. In any case, the ability to mobilize this sub-process can be a competitive advantage in many industry segments.

Step 4: Calculate the M index for the Industry Type

With an understanding of the importance of the supply chain mega processes to your business segment and the relationship of mobility to each process, you can begin to calculate the M index for your company. We recommend a three-stage process.

First, assign a degree of mobility reliance to each of the supply chain mega process based on the industry's segment. For example, the commodity nature of in the Grow to Market (G2M) environment (agriculture and produce), gives the planning function a relatively low level of importance. So the Plan component would be assigned a rating of low/medium (L/M), which translates to a score of 2 as shown below. Similarly, Buy would receive a low/medium score as the input materials tend to be relatively static and well managed, and the associated supply base mostly local. The Make—or in this case, really the Grow—component is highly relevant for this industry segment. Therefore, Make is given a high (H) rating as is Sell/Service because of the daily customer-intensive nature of this segment. Move gets an in between rating of medium/high (M/H), given the perishable nature and short shelf life of many of the products.

Table 1 below shows the ratings for Grow-to-market as well as sample rating for the other industry segments.

TABLE: UNSHACKLED PART XII

Segment/ Degree of Reliance	Plan	Buy	Make	Move	Sell/ Serve
MTS	H (5)	M/H (4)	M/H (4)	M/H (4)	M/H (4)
ATO	M/H (4)	M/H (4)	M (3)	M (3)	H (5)
BTO	L/M (2)	M/H (4)	M/H (4)	M (3)	H (5)
G2M	L/M (2)	L/M (2)	H (5)	M/H (4)	H (5)

Table 1: Mega Process Ratings for Segments

Assume that High (H) = 5 points; Medium (M) = 3 points and Low (L) = 1 point. M/L is 4 points and L/M is 2 points.

The second stage shown in Table 2 uses the same scoring construct as the one above but applies it in terms of mobility's relative applicability to each of the mega processes—regardless of industry type. As discussed earlier in the article, the Plan, Buy and Make processes are lower on the mobility applicability scale than are the Move and Sell processes. Therefore, Plan, Buy and Make are given a L/M score (2 points); Move and Sell/Service receive a M/H rating, or 4 points.

TABLE: UNSHACKLED PART XII

Table 2: Importance of M to Mega Processes

Supply Chain Process	Mobility Process
Plan	L/M (2)
Buy	L/M (2)
Make	L/M (2)
Move	M/H (4)
Sell/ Serve	M/H (4)

The final stage takes the scoring in the first two steps to derive the composite score for each segment. The composite score is the industry segment mega process (Table 1) times the Mobility importance score (Table 2).

Finally, to derive the Mobility index, divide the composite score by the maximum possible score of 125 (ratings of 5 across all processes and a 5 rating on mobility importance) to derive the mobility index for the industry segment. Table 4 shows the M Index for each segment type:

TABLE: UNSHACKLED PART XII

Table 4: M Index by Segment		
Segment Type	M Index (total score/125)	Sample Industry Association
MTS	0.47	Consumer Products, Electronics, Chemicals, Pharmaceuticals, Automotive
ATO	0.43	High Technology (hardware), Semiconductor
BTO	0.42	Engineering and Construction, Heavy Manufacturing, Aerospace and Defense
G2M	0.43	Agriculture

The M scores in general are not very high. Make to Stock, which scored highest on the M Index, came in at a little under 0.5. The findings suggest that while opportunities exist to gain cost and service benefits from mobility, the case for adoption needs to be carefully considered. The findings further suggest that the adoption curve will tend to be fairly slow. Adoption likely will not proceed in a single sweep across all processes, but will follow a sequential approach—for example, distribution first, followed by transportation, and so on. Importantly, we are not asserting that mobility in the supply chain processes is in any way unnecessary or undesirable. Rather, we believe that the use of mobility will continue to be spot based and sporadic across the industry segments and will not necessarily be a candidate for massive adoption and rollouts.

STRUCTURED IMPLEMENTATION APPROACH

If a decision is made to move forward on a mobility initiative, we recommend the following structured approach. It consists of four activities—define, select, implement, and monitor. (See Exhibit 2.)

Following this methodology will enhance the potential of capturing the benefits of M.

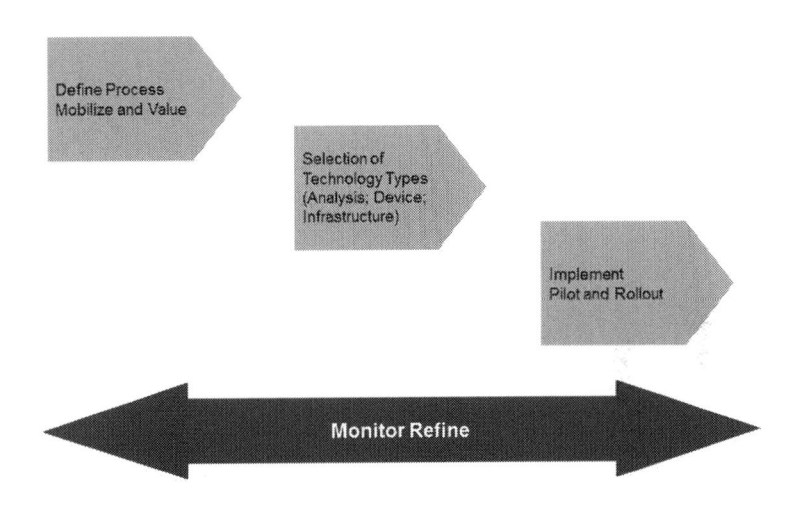

```
[Define Process Mobilize and Value] → [Selection of Technology Types (Analysis; Device; Infrastructure)] → [Implement Pilot and Rollout]
← Monitor Refine →
```

Exhibit 2: Mobility Implementation Approach

Define. The first step is to define the process and associated sub-processes that are proposed candidates for mobility. We suggest utilizing some variation of the SCOR (Supply Chain Operations Reference) model or a derivative that accurately describes the company's supply chain operating model. It is important to carefully define the candidate processes and sub-processes since we have seen the variation in results and applicability even within the mega process. We also suggest mobilizing the implementation team—which should include the business process owner, IT, and data security professionals—at this stage. Finally, a key output of this step is creation of a value generation and delivery model that will enable a reasonable ROI. (Reasonableness of ROI's would be determined based on the company's internal hurdle rates for financial investments.)

Select. The next step is to select the technology enablers. These can be classified in three categories: devices, back-end infrastructure, and rendering platform.

Regarding the first category, a wide selection of devices now is available from companies like Apple, Samsung, HP, RIM, and more. The choice of device can often be coupled with selection of back-end operating and storage technology (MS/Mac/CE) as well as the integration technology required to connect the devices to the infrastructure. The market has yet to shake out and it will likely be at least four to five years before clear winners and losers emerge. The final piece of the puzzle is the rendering and business process analytics layer. This platform is used to deliver the M capability and receive the results back from any process/data manipulation that may have been done by the front-line users. (We note here that mobility without interactivity and analytics is really useless.) Once again, there are many platforms available from business intelligence providers as well as providers of analytic capabilities. The main output of this step is the creation of a technology roadmap that supports results of the "Define" step.

Implement. The third step in the process is to implement the enablers selected above. Before any large scale employment across the processes and sub-processes, however, we encourage the use of pilot launches and tests. This will enable the company and the front-line users to adapt and adopt the changes in the business process and technology enablers for optimal benefit. Remember, for people using the M technology, there's big shift in operating model and mindset from a "batch" to "real time." So there are change management issues that need to be dealt with.

Monitor and Refine. The fourth and last step is often forgotten in many technology-centric business process transformations. Yet, it's crucial to monitor and refine the sub process and associated usage since the adopting of mobility typically is a learning experience in and of itself—that is, users learn more as they work with the technology and become more adept in utilizing analytics and applying the results to drive decisions. Hence, we recommend a bimonthly review-and-refine process for at least six months after initial implementation. A company's M index is defined largely by its supply chain operating philosophy as well as the particular industry segment to which belongs. From our vantage point, the use of mobility in the supply chain is still in its early stages and the M index scores we posited demonstrate why widespread adoption has not already occurred. There are, however, a number of ways in which the early adopters can gain significant advantage. As the value proposition becomes clearer going forward, expect to see more and more companies embracing M.

A Practitioner's Take on Mobility

One company that we have worked with, Niagara Bottling Co., has already begun to capture the value potential in mobility. The California-based firm has been in business since 1963.

Niagara's advancements in vertical integration, innovative bottle design, and high-speed manufacturing positioned the company as the industry leading family owned and operated bottled water supplier in the United States. Ashley Dorna, the company's Executive Vice President, Supply Chain Management for the past decade, has been integral in helping Niagara adopt new and emerging technologies to drive supply chain excellence. One of those initiatives centers on mobility.

Dorna explains: "We are heavily focused on integrating mobility into our supply chain. As we continue to grow at a breakneck pace in a dynamic and fluid environment, we are finding that leveraging mobile platforms is critical in enabling the frontline worker to be more agile and efficient in their daily activities. Our goals of driving facility throughput and increased customer satisfaction can only be achieved by leaving the desktop and manual decision making behind and embracing mobility."

Canaan Reich, Niagara's senior Information Technology executive and Director of IT, agrees with Dorna. Mr. Reich has led business enablement centric technology projects at Niagara over the last five years, many with a mobility component.

Says Mr. Reich "All of our current business process design and improvements focus on minimizing the amount of manual work required by our employees. As much as possible, we are shifting from repetitive activities to exception based handling. Improved mobility gains importance when empowering personnel with real time decision making."

NOTES FROM CHAPTER

UNSHACKLED PART XIII

Deciding the Core and Non-Core – A page from mathematics

Axioms and PQ

In the field of mathematics, we have two types of statements. One is called an axiom and the other is called a theorem. An axiom is a statement that does not need to be proven and is accepted as the "truth," and a theorem is one that needs rigorous proof. If we draw a parallel in today's global and connected economy, the axiom of the new economy could simply be stated as "Excel in your core areas of strength and partner for the rest." This is a far different type of environment than one that existed even a decade back. Today we hear about companies outsourcing or partnering in areas of information services; back office functions like payroll, accounts payable, and receivable; human-factors management; engineering and design services; procurement; logistics; and so on. The list grows larger and more innovative every day.

It is not unfathomable to envision a day in which some of our activities have been pre- or post-processed in some remote part of the world, by a resource that knows us purely by a number and has no personal touch into our daily routine. We are already faced with some of that in claims processing as well as the hallowed land of medicine in which MRI reports and pathology laboratory reports are being read in India and diagnoses are being sent across the www.world for delivery in North America.

If we accept the axiom that vertical integration for all functions and services is not a sustainable value proposition in today's extended economy, then it begs the question of what methods can be used to determine the core areas of focus for a company as well as what metrics are needed to govern the behaviors and actions of partners.

There is never a cookie cutter solution or a one-size-fits-all environment for all industries or functions. Having worked in consumer products, retail, high technology, as well as the automotive industry, I am still trying to find the panacea that everyone can be happy with. Unfortunately, it does not exist. However, we can still find some core patterns and frameworks that can be applied to a somewhat nebulous process. However, we have found that frameworks applied in isolation cannot be successful or implementable. To make a framework useful, I have always found that a balanced scorecard approach to verifying and validating certain decisions as well as answering the multimillion-dollar question "To partner or not to partner?" The remainder of this article focuses on putting forth a point of view on these topics that have worked well in the industry. It is by no means the only approach or the panacea, but is one approach to answering a question that is complex, multidimensional, and extremely relevant in today's globally connected economy.

Before launching into a discussion around a framework that logically extends the segmentation of work effort and cash flow that we introduced in Chapter Two, we should spend some time discussing the subtle nuances that are inherently imbedded, and tends to distract transformational efforts, in the political quotient (PQ) of any corporation. We define PQ of any corporation as the aptitude of the personnel to turn a transformational or change effort into a series of miniature political dramatics that each has a set of central characters jockeying for some self-fulfilling positions or counterproductive propositions to the one that is being pursued under the change umbrella. I have worked with a number of global corporations in which the senior executives would put to vote decisions that did not require any democratic approval by middle management. This was often done under the guise of wanting to achieve consensus in the ranks but ended up being an exercise to satisfy the lowest common denominator (LCD) amongst the set of naysayers. This method can immediately subtract from the C.O.L.E. benefits since transformational efforts are never intended to satisfy the LCD of a process or set of processes. More often than not, transformations will attack the cumulative effect of the LCDs that add up to the set of inherent inefficiencies in the processes. My personal bias tends to center around ensuring that senior executives provide firm and unwavering support for any transformation. Without that guarantee, it is unlikely that any effort will ever succeed. In fact, we can say that the probability of success is inversely proportional to the PQ of a corporation.

$$Pr(S^T) \approx PQ^{-1}$$

Having said that, we should note that no transformational effort will be devoid of some element of PQ and the trick is to channel the energy and focus of the organization along the correct dimensions.

ALIGNMENT TO CORE AND NON-CORE

Complexity (Risk/reward)
High
Low

Alignment to Core
Low   High

Figure One: Complexity Tradeoffs

One framework that I have applied at companies with a clear definition and understanding of their core value proposition is shown above. The various processes and work streams that are needed to conduct commerce within a corporation can be bucketed based on the closeness to the core. We have to be very careful in defining what core competencies are for a corporation. It is not just an exercise in activities and processes that we have developed and gained competencies in, but is a snap shot of the activities that ensures a high degree of customer intimacy. Many argue that anything that even touches the customer needs to be bucketed under intimacy, but I would argue that there are processes that are customer centric but can be easily managed with governance and do not have to be conducted by the corporation. A great example of this is transportation and warehousing. Both these processes impact customer service but can easily be governed by the corporation and performed by an expert provider,i.e., 3PLs. In similar fashion, many companies partner up for the process of external customer service (not B2B but B2C). It is also commonplace to hear about various companies shifting their call centers from partners back in house,[1] but very few of these companies have taken the time to figure out that the external call center personnel are only as good as the change management and training programs that they are immersed in. It is the joint responsibility of the host company to execute the training program with the same degree of rigor that they would use to train their internal constituents.

Complexity in Figure One is defined as the risk to reward ratio that can be derived by migrating away from status quo for the current delivery options that exist for the process or group of processes. This ratio should be explicitly documented and calculated since many corporations tend to focus on the reward at the start of the transformation and only the risks after the initial euphoria has worn off. We should also caution that risk should not be confused by operational noise in the system (see Chapter One), but should be tabulated as the broad risk categories like geo-political, economic, human capital transition, and so on.

The higher the alignment or contribution to the core proposition, the greater the chances that they will be mapped in the lower right and upper right hand box. The others will be listed on the left hand side of the matrix to indicate that a company would benefit from in the event that a partnering decision is made. It is highly unlikely that a company would partner for the activities along the right hand side of the quadrant. If the processes are "commodity like," that is, easily available globally, then the cost of ownership becomes quite the deciding factor. However, if the process is aligned to the core but has a low level of complexity, that is, risk is low and reward is high, then one has to define the expected quality of the work and metrics that are needed to measure the effectiveness of a global partner.

	Process Classification - Optimize internally first	Process Classification - Focus internally
H	Decision criterion - Price based	Supply Chain Management
		Brand Management
Complexity (Risk/reward)		Channel Management
	Process Classification – Commodity	Process Classification – Almost "Commodity"
	Decision criterion - Price based	Decision criterion – Price and quality
		Information Services
		Customer Service
		Logistics

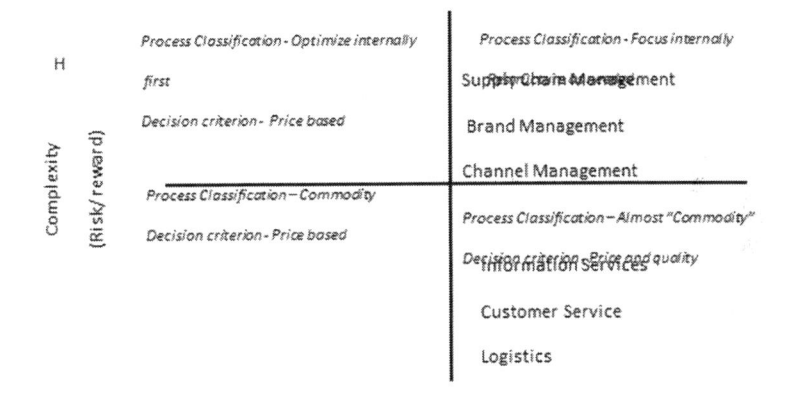

Figure Two: Process and Operating criterion matrix

In Figure Two, we provide a segmentation approach from the FMCG industry segment that can be used as a starting point for discussions around the final operating model for any corporation. While it is not clear why processes that eventually find their into the lower left quadrant should remain within the day-to-day execution and management of a corporation, it is also not a slam dunk that those processes that are in the top right quadrant should always be completely retained within the corporation as part of the final operating model. There are very few "black and white" answers in the design of the operating model; there are a lot of industry indicators as well as best practices that can be used to serve as guidelines for an eventual operating model blueprint. The decision criterion that is presented in the matrix is intended to serve as an indicator for the focus that should be put on the discussion with potential partners. A price-based discussion normally indicates the presence of multiple global providers for the processes in question as well as the ability to extract the right level of commoditized value over the lifecycle of the contract. In similar fashion, price and quality implies that while multiple suppliers are available, it is quite important to aggressively manage the potential changeover disruptions that are caused by switching suppliers due to the alignment of the process with the proposed core of the corporation. The top two quadrants suggest a slightly modified evolution process with a focus on being more focused on deriving portions of C.O.L.E internally prior to generating additional leverage brought to the table by an outside partner.

An example application of the framework is a generic high-end branded, fast-moving manufacturing company (Figure Two) that has to deal with the consistent pressure on gross margins as well as ever-increasing demands for innovation from the channel and the end consumer. The aim is to figure out areas that are potentially available for global partnering as well as continue to shift costs from "commodity like" activity to the higher end value generating activities that will alleviate the pressures on margin.

It is a well known fact that the continued aim for companies that are looking to stay competitive as well as thrive in the economy of constant margin pressures as well as continued shift in the power between the manufacturers and retailers in the quest to "own the end consumer." Both parties would like to be in a situation where their own physical or cyber assets are the destination for the feet or the eyeball. The continued sources of co-opetition arise from the sheer fact that both enterprises would like to believe that the end consumer's choice of destination is driven primarily by the power of either the retail or the cyber brand and not by the product assortment that is provided. Similarly, the manufacturing entities would like to believe that the power of the brand is what entices the ever-expanding share of the consumer's wallet. As is the case of most channel and product debates that will rage on forever, the truth lies somewhere in the middle.

However, there is a growing list of world class companies and a list of equally large set of partners[1] that are providing commodity services in a globally leveraged and highly optimized fashion

DECIDING THE CORE AND NON-CORE – A PAGE FROM MATHEMATICS

around all areas in the bottom two quadrants. The degree to which these services are delivered on-site vs. remote, the level of partnering, the exact portions of the process that are suitable for partnering, and so on, are all detailed questions that have to be answered prior to a transformational launch. We will address many of the questions in the later chapters of this book as well.

While the debate continues, both ends of the value chain in every industry as well as all value-added partners in the middle, have to continue to manage the global dynamics around the fundamental law of business mathematics, that is, Profit – Cost = Margin. In many instances, forces in the global markets as opposed to the channel partners or the product manufacturers are setting the margin figure. The recent phenomenon of fixed margins has now forced the channel to adjust its business models to manage the profit and cost equation more aggressively. This has given rise to renewed emphasis and elevation of disciplines such as supply chain management as well as customer relationship management. However, as many global companies are finding out the fact that it is not enough to just focus on material and logistics cost or the cost of service for the end product, but every cost item that is used to deliver the product and service. These other cost elements that are primarily considered as part of general and administrative (the G&A of SG&A) are now an emerging area of focus under the new field called Business Process Optimization or sometimes called Business Process Outsourcing (BPO).

A Quick Word on BPO

What is business process outsourcing? Business process outsourcing otherwise known as BPO is the process of leveraging technology vendors in various cost and labor advantaged third world or developing nations for doing a job which was once the responsibility of the corporation. Or simply put, it is the process of shifting an internal job process to an outside/external company, which might have a completely different geographical location.

Generally, the processes being outsourcing as part of BPO are back-end jobs like call/help centers, medical transcription, billing, payroll processing, data entry, human resource management, and the like. Most of these jobs are outsourcing by first world nations like the USA and UK to third world nations like India, Philippines, China, Malaysia, and some eastern European countries. These nations have a good pool of English speaking graduates who receive language and accent neutralization accent and job related training before they are inducted at a salary, which is much lesser than what their counterparts in first world nations would demand. This allows global corporations to get higher profits and provide better services by lowering the prices and by recruiting more labor than they could possibly do otherwise. In addition to benefiting global corporations, BPO has also benefited third world nations by generating much needed jobs.

Factor	Weight (between 0 and 1 and adds to 1)	Importance (H = 3; M = 2; L=1)
Delivery model of the service i.e. on site vs. self service vs. off site		
Quality of current service vs. desired quality		
Price of current service vs. future (include upgrades and quality)		
Flexibility desired (time spent vs. focus vs. cost)		
Industry knowledge required to perform service		
Openness of company to inter and intra company problem resolutions		

Figure Three: A Sample Scorecard

As Thomas Friedman states in his best-selling book, *The World is Flat*,[2] the rapid convergence and proliferation of extensible Technologies across the globe has shrunk the world into Globalization 3.0, in which The World is Flat.

THE SCORECARD

Over the years, our professional experiences allow us to create our own portfolio of business dos and don'ts or watch outs. Sometimes these are colored by our own propensity to take risks as well as, in many instances, the management philosophy of the corporation. If we took some time to put our own portfolio on a piece of paper, it will probably look similar to the one that I listed below as criterion that can be used to evaluate various functions in the company's internal value chain. One sample scorecard that I often use to illustrate to senior management the various options that are available is as follows:

Factor is the criterion that is used to evaluate the function, or in the case of outsourcing, the outsourcer; weight is the relative measure between the factors; importance is a differentiator amongst factors of the same weight (in many cases, we can combine the weight and importance columns).

While most of the factors are self-explanatory, I would like to point out the importance of the openness factor, also measured as the company culture, to having remote services or partner provided services provided in the overall evaluation criterion of the decision to in-source or outsource. Too often, the price equation becomes the overriding criterion that is used to arrive at a decision. However, this provides short-term gains and many times the pain of the process is not worth the effort. Similarly, the effect of automation and technology advances in driving down the overall cost without having to outsource should also be factored in, as well as the internal ability to create global delivery models that can provide some levels of cost savings without having to bring in external providers. These are delicate tradeoffs that require careful analysis and internal retrospection of the company's senior management in order to decide what functions truly makes up the core of the corporation. Remember the scorecard is used to further refine what functions remain under the category that we have called "distraction."

Top Five Journey Pointers

So, if you have managed to steer the company's management team to the point at which the journey to partner with a service provider is imminent, you may want to consider some of these areas since they have worked for me and many other practitioners:

1. <u>Change Management</u> is as a key ingredient for eventual success. In many efforts, we shortchange the change management effort around communication, training, and alignment of the many facets of the company around the effort. I cannot emphasize enough the razor sharp focus around all aspects of change management that is required to be successful. One veteran practitioner once told me that it was paramount that one receives at a minimum "grudging support" for any outsourcing effort from all the functional and divisional heads in the corporation in order to succeed.

2. <u>Don't cut too deep</u>: As with any transformation effort, the type of business model or delivery model that is used to staff the future world is key to the success. In my experience, cutting to the bone and hollowing out the organization will not deliver the type of long-term sustainable results that are needed to achieve continued innovation in every function.

3. <u>If in doubt, retain in-house:</u> While this sounds a little clichéd, it actually holds true for the future operating model nuances of any process. If executive consensus process truly leaves a particular process design "on the fence," it may be a worthwhile sustainable exercise to either revisit the exact criterion that are causing doubt or just delay the execution of the process for the new operating model while allowing the corporation to adjust to change. This does not mean that we are driving change by consensus or propagating habits that are inherently sub optimal for the corporation—we are just building further confidence in our ability to drive a truly sustainable change process by generating small victories along the way.

4. <u>An "ERP" solution is not always optimal</u>: In the age of the ERP software suites where we have been conditioned to think that best of breed increases the total cost of ownership, many providers would like us to apply the same logic to outsourcing. I have found that economies of scale do exist in many instances but have to be traded off against the risk of being too dependent on one provider. I have preached and will continue to preach the concept of dual provider sourcing for a company, preferably not within a business function or process but across functions and processes. The total

cost of ownership equation when dampened by the risk mitigation factor can be quite revealing.

5. <u>Aim, aim, test, test, and then test again before you fire</u>: Sounds quite obvious, does it not? You will be amazed at the number of companies that do not have a well-defined pilot and test plan prior to turning on the process to the outsourcers. This is often a cause of mismanaged deals and expectations that result in the much publicized breakages that we read about in the popular press. Just like a large software implementation, the end result is only as good as the test scripts that are used to test the package. Expect that bugs will always exist, but the onus is on both parties to test the obvious scenarios that will result in high-severity impacts to the business.

Summary

While concluding this section, I would like to remind the readers that there is no single approach or solution that works for all situations that we may encounter. Every situation is probably quite unique in the fact that there are slight nuances that makes the framework and the examples null and void. I would encourage all of us to have a framework as well as a balanced scorecard while evaluating these strategic shifts in a company's future. One thing is for certain, the lack of a systematic approach to these problems will result in total failures—and that is an axiom.

Portions of this Chapter were adapted from the article "Global Partnering for success" by the author in Silicon India magazine in March 2005. See www.siliconindia.com

NOTES FROM CHAPTER

UNSHACKLED PART XIV

Ten New Ideas for Generating Supply Chain Value

Innovatiol1 is the lifeblood of all companies. This could be in the form of new products, services or even new operating models. In the absence of innovation, a company will face the certain "death by commoditization" effect over a period of time. Yet where the supply chain is concerned, innovation seems to be lacking in all too many cases. It is rare to find an organization thinking about- let alone investing in- supply chain innovation. However, they will readily spend hundreds of millions of dollars on product and service innovation.

Why is this the case? Why does investment in supply chain process innovation lag so far behind the growth and strategic importance of the function? To find some answers, I revisited a prior chapter titled "The Top Ten Supply Chain Mistakes.". It's evident that many companies across industries are still making those mistakes. They remain slow to adopt even basic best practices to leverage the supply chain's power. So if they are still struggling with the fundamentals, it's not surprising that they haven't given much thought to innovation.

But by not embracing innovation companies foreclose on an important opportunity to add value to their business and to their supply chain. This article sets forth ten innovative supply chain ideas that can add value. They can lead to positive outcomes in any economic environment. Applied aggressively during turbulent economic times like these, however, they can yield powerful results that will position companies well for the upturn we hope and expect to come.

Ten Innovative Ideas

The ten value-adding ideas presented here will be reflected in different parts of the P&L and balance sheets, as we describe below. Exhibit 1 groups the ideas, some of which overlap, into three broad impact areas-revenue enhancement, cost management, and sustainability.

While management buy-in and cross-functional coordination are essential to making these ideas work, they all reside squarely in the domain of the supply chain function and its managers.

Idea One: Shift the focus from order-to-delivery to design-to-support

We've all spent endless months (and sometime years) focusing supply chain management on the order-to-delivery (OTD) process. This made inherent sense since OTD represents 15 to 25 percent of the supply chain variable cost in the typical company. Over the years, many companies have developed strong competencies in the traditional activities of Plan, Buy, Make, and Move, which are geared to planning and delivering with sustained excellence. In the face of constantly escalating commodity pricing and a decrease in immediately available substitute sources of supply, however, many companies have found that the cost drivers have shifted to the product design and bill of material structures.

Recently, we were engaged in two fairly lengthy discussions with the heads of global operations for a consumer health care and a medical device company. Both companies are global in their customer and supply base. In addition to sharing common supply chain challenges, both these executives had one common goal: To change the product design process to adapt to the shifting commodity pricing market. The two executives both were focused on driving their entire design and research team to explore alternate materials that would not lock them into the current commodity cost structure. They were spending less of their time and innovation budget looking into alternate sourcing models for current products and more on exploring alternate design materials that would also positively impact post-production support, including parts and spares management.

The Design-to-Delivery Framework

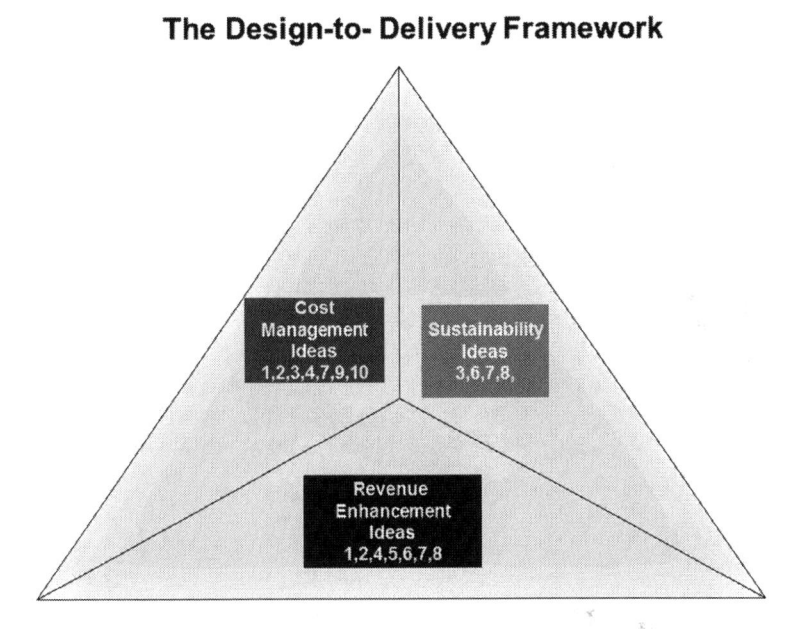

Exhibit 1: Impact areas of the 10 Ideas

- Cost Management Ideas: 1,2,3,4,7,9,10
- Sustainability Ideas: 3,6,7,8
- Revenue Enhancement Ideas: 1,2,4,5,6,7,8

The whole concept of design-driven manufacturing and alternate bill of material structure, though long overlooked, is capturing new attention these days-and with good reason. Shifting the focus to design-to-support will enable companies to fully explore their inherent strengths in product design and innovation while continuing to drive down supply chain costs. However, this shift will necessitate the adoption of lean and agile manufacturing principles that emphasize rapid prototyping and speed to market, which also means achieving the right mix of agility with stability that we have always strived for in our supply chain practices.

Idea Two: Look for hidden values in reverse logistics

The reverse value chain has traditionally been treated as more of a compliance and regulatory issue than a generator of value or competitive advantage. Yet reverse logistics costs as a percent of revenue can range between 3 and 6 percent, depending on the type of industry and product. Returns can range widely-from 4 percent all the way up to 50 percent in the publishing industry, for example. Obviously, returns represent a prime source for discovering significant value that can immediately drop to the bottom line.

Some cellular network providers, for example, have gained sustained startup cost advantages by offering refurbished or remanufactured phone sets at a fraction of the cost of the new equipment. These efforts have been driven by a well-executed return and manufacturing process for equipment that is not at end of life.

As corporations increasingly adopt green initiatives as a core part of the value chain, they find that component refurbishing and reuse can be a source of additional value. This approach, coupled with the right set of controls for reusable products such as wooden pallets that are traditionally considered disposable, can positively impact the cost basis by a factor of 1 to 3 percentage points.

A well-constructed reverse logistics framework includes the following components: a dedicated returns network that is separate from the company's forward network processes designed specifically for the reuse and reverse logistics activities; incentives for the dealer/retail network to perform value-added services such as efficiently sending back damaged product or incorrect orders; and predictive tools and technologies to accurately predict inventory velocity needed to ensure customer satisfaction. As a competitive lever, appropriate cost drivers for the reverse logistics effort also must be in place.

Idea Three: Globalize the functional processes and adopt a "follow the sun" model for skill deployment

Information technology outsourcing has become mainstream over the past 15 to 20 years. The global delivery model for outsourced IT services has migrated from on-site to "right-shore" – based on cost, skills and technology availability. It is commonplace to have a U.S.-based company's help desk call answered in Philippines with a back up agent in Ireland and remote services for desktop support coming from India. This taps into the English speaking skills in the Philippines, the tax advantages of a location like Ireland, and the technical skill base and good bandwidth available in India.

We have not seen the application of similar thinking applied to supply chain processes such as planning, procurement, customer service, and innovation. These resource-intensive activities could benefit from a careful analysis of what might outsourced or "right shored".

There are four simple steps to accomplish this.

1. Create the "task pyramid". Every supply chain process can be segmented into the following task hierarchy and assigned a percentage of time spent on each: administrative, analytical, and innovative and cross functional. Take normal supply chain planning functional processes, which include demand management activities; supply and manufacturing planning; new product commercialization cross processes; customer service and sales cross functional processes.

2. Specify the lead times required to perform the processes and elapsed time necessary to perform the associated tasks. This suggests that all associated tasks are performed to add specific value for the product or the services that the company is providing.

3. Find logical breakpoints in the process. With demand planning, for example, these breakpoints could be process mapping and analysis, data analysis, data socialization and realignment based on inputs from cross functional groups, and commitment to plan. Each of the task segments listed above has a logical breakpoint and, hence, can be treated as a self-contained segment.

4. For the various task segments, create a "right shore" map that is balanced against the associated lead time boundaries. This will lead to extracting the best use of global skills that are available within the company or with partners that can provide the required process services.

Utilizing the simple four-step approach will ensure that the company is globalizing the supply chain functional processes as well as utilizing the talent pools that are available across the world. This will enable creation of functional centers of excellence across the organization's geographic span while freeing up overburdened resources to now execute the required supply chain process.

Idea Four: Manage the supply chain using the concept of floor-and-surge to deliver with increased agility and less waste

In the *Supply Chain Management Review* article mentioned earlier, we discussed the concept of having multiple supply chains within a company. Today, that concept may be more relevant than ever as companies balance the need to be market responsive against ever escalating total landed supply chain costs.

Companies still tend to operate one supply chain and manage all end-to-end activities using the same level of rigor-or lack thereof. Decisions are made primarily using manufacturing cost as the primary determinant, with the major tradeoffs typically between lead times and safety stock. Yet in today's dynamic, consumer-driven market, where forecasting is always risky, lead times vary widely, and safety stock is extremely costly, this traditional approach may not be best.

We suggest using the floor-and-surge capacity model as a more responsive alternative. Through this approach, the company invests in load leveled ("floor") capacity for the stable and fast-moving products, also known as high flow-through products. These are products that move very quickly and repetitively through the supply chain in extremely cost advantaged locations since lead times can be buffered by setting appropriate safety stock policies.

For the products that have more variable demand patterns, are candidates for postponement techniques (pack size variations, color variations, or other variations that does not disturb the basic configuration), or are seasonal or promotion-intensive, we recommend a "surge" approach. These products are planned and produced separately from the more stable demand products. In many instances the surge manufacturing is co-located with the floor manufacturing arena; however, it is managed in a more agile manner. Depending on the product's characteristics, one may consider deferring end production of surge products as near to the end channel/consumer as possible (for example, in postponement centers).

The flow-and-surge approach allows the corporation to benefit from the longer production run economics as well as the labor arbitrage that many seek.

Idea Five: Focus on real-time updates and adjustments to increase agility and shape responsiveness. (Traditional static forecasting without dynamic updates is passé.)

Senior manufacturing executives frequently ask, "Is forecasting necessary? Is it relevant in a day when product life spans are getting shorter and consumer preferences are becoming even more fickle? Is the traditional view of demand planning dead?" Our view is that planning and forecasting is still necessary. Yet it now needs to be conducted in near-real time.

What does it mean to be near-real time? It's the minimum time required to provide supply chain stability with respect to necessary manufacturing lead time and the necessary transportation lead time. In today's dynamic environment, you nee-m to dynamically adjust the plan based on real-time market signals such as point-of-sale data, purchase order activity, and competitive market factors. Many find it hard to think through the implementation of the concept because of the deep-rooted notion that planning horizons are monthly and required to provide manufacturing stability. This traditional thinking has led to continued higher-than-necessary inventory levels across the entire extended supply chain (including the suppliers) as well as customer service levels that are still stagnating in the mid-80 percent.

However, if you couple Idea Four (floor-and-surge) with a real-time dynamic planning horizon, it leads to a much higher degree of agility. Additionally, the tendency to focus on snap shots of monthly demand numbers often leads to high levels of dampening of the "within week and within month" customer order variations. We would propose that companies think about the total demand that would be consumed within a certain time period (lifecycle) and use the dynamic predictability concept to project the entire lifecycle (amount that will be sold or shipped during a certain time period such as a holiday program) to augment the baseline static forecast. Done on a weekly basis, such augmentation will prevent the high error levels and variations often found in many industries.

The agricultural produce industry offers a great example of the dynamic nature of demand management. The normal modes of demand planning are almost irrelevant because of the huge impact of the weather on the produce that is harvested. Complicating this are yield issues, and size and color variations of the produce. The end result is that predicting demand beyond a week becomes almost impossible. This industry uses daily demand and supply management to ship product across the country to the various retail channels. The industry leaders exhibit the ultimate agility in adapting and shaping demand patterns based on available product.

Idea Six: Redefine the traditional supply chain silos and culture to make it value chain-centric and hence ensure a more successful product launch

The supply chain function in most corporations is initiated and integrated at the time of new product commercialization and continues until the product is shipped. This is a huge step from even a decade earlier when the functions of manufacturing, procurement and shipping were mainly viewed in isolation. Integration of the supply chain functions, which is fast becoming commonplace, has delivered huge benefits in both COGS and income statement measures for many companies.

Two key critical activities, however, have been left out of this integrative process: product design planning and direct relationships with channel partners and customers. In most cases today, the supply chain function picks up when the product design is completed and initial costs have been approved. However, the supply chain should be involved right after the initial idea-generation process has been completed. This will allow the companies to more effectively assess alternate design specifications in light of availability and location of supplies. It would also enable the supply chain management to identify potential supply channels and identify alternate materials as well as supply networks. In the end, this involvement would result in a better cost platform for the new product.

The second area that supply chain management professionals needs to expand into is in dealing with and forging direct relationships with channel partners and customers. The traditional supply chain function typically ended when the product was shipped and again picked up if there were issues with missed shipments or product returns. However, as the supply chain has become strategic to both the manufacturer and the channel partner, it needs to proactively plan for and address operational issues vs. reacting to them. Forging the direct relationships to augment the existing ones typically held and nurtured by the sales function will yield a smoother product positioning (for new products); greater agility to deal with out-of-stock situations; and the ability to work jointly to reduce total landed costs as well create value in innovating in category management type of activities.

Idea Seven: Create demand and supply pools for commodity products and services that extend the normal span of enterprise focus

We were recently speaking with the senior management teams from three different corporations ranging in annual revenues from $400 million to $3 billion. None of these companies had competing products, either existing or planned. However, each of the companies was spending large amounts of effort, personnel and associated technology in managing demand and supply for what could be considered commodity products and services (i.e., those not differentiating from a product or company value). These included MRO spend; non-strategic marketing spend; non-strategic product spend like shrink wrap and corrugated, and so forth.

As the discussion progressed, my thoughts went back to 2001, when many of us were discussing the entire concept of B2B exchanges. The aim of B2B exchanges was to lower the spend level in these commoditized areas. The problem was that results too often fell short of expectations, and the B2B exchange idea largely fell out of favor.

Yet today many companies are once again beginning to work with members of the extended value community in pooling their spend and in systematically driving greater consolidation across the supply chain while improving service and in many cases lowering total cost of ownership (this includes not just the piece price but also associated personnel, process and technology costs). We are not advocating the re-emergence of B2B exchanges. Instead, we're saying that companies should continually seek to manage their commodity spend by exploring means of partnerships and participation in concepts such as pooling and spend leverage.

Idea Eight: Shift the focus of supply chain management from product only to product and services management

Our traditional focus, particularly in the manufacturing environment, has been on the various aspects of product excellence. Now, more and more companies are adding an element of value added services to create "stickiness" with their channel partners. The supply chain should take note. This does
not mean that the supply chain should become a direct provider of value-added services into the marketplace. Instead, we're suggesting that the function adopt a strong element of a service in its mindset and day-to-day execution. This includes all components of the supply chain-planning, sourcing and procurement, transportation and logistics, and so forth.

This service orientation also should be extended to the channel partners as well as strategic suppliers. The aim here is to optimize the end-to-end supply chain process. This could involve the establishment of value added services like CPFR (collaborative planning, forecasting and replenishment); VMI (vendor managed inventory); and collaborative and joint business planning. It could also entail the creation of best-practice sharing centers of excellence. Joint educational programs that address the significant value of working together would be valuable in this regard as well.

This mindset and cultural shift required to implement this idea is easier said than done. It involves a fundamental migration from a internally focused mindset to one that is more consultative and collaborative. This type of shift often calls for a significant change management effort among personnel as well as augmentation of current skills with external resources. The payoff associated with making this shift, however, will be evident in increased customer service levels and marked improvements in product flow-through.

Idea Nine: Utilize on-demand process and associated supporting technology to complement existing investments

Many companies have invested in the traditional people, process and technology aspects of the business. Where the supply chain is concerned, there's been a particular emphasis on the so-called enabling technology. Yet none of us need or want another study that is based on the clever use of analytics and huge spread sheet-based models that is not followed up with a robust implementation plan. We all know that any implementation plan will have large elements of technology. However, we are also entering an era in which large capital investments will be scrutinized extremely closely due to the tightening of the credit markets and expenditures for other areas of investments like property, plant and equipment (PP&E).

We suggest that companies take a closer look at using on-demand processes and technologies across the value chain. This approach will allow for the optimal usage of capital expenditures while leading to higher than average adoption rates of the process in order to derive maximum benefit. On-demand enablers are now widely available from most Tier 1 and Tier 2 technology vendors and have been gaining significant ground in recent years. Such solutions are no longer limited to the well-known on-demand technology for sales called salesforce.com.

Many companies are beginning to utilize this approach for advanced processes like detailed analytics that may not be required on a regular basis or for advanced capabilities like network and warehouse design. Several providers have made available on-demand models for these types of activities (as opposed to the traditional project based offering). A number of companies (including ours) provide deep analytical services using a follow-the-sun model from cost advantaged locations like India and emerging areas like Latin America. Expect to see these types of services becoming more mainstream in the next few years as the focus continues on cost restructuring and "doing more with less."

Idea Ten: Decide on the right level of value chain responsiveness, then apply the "Rule of 5 percent."

Responsiveness is critical to the market success. One recent survey found the difference between market leaders and laggards was their ability to respond to ever-changing market conditions.

Responsiveness should be viewed as complement to lean. In a recent discussion I had with an automotive executive, he made the comment that his company had become too lean and could no longer be as responsive.

Every organization should take stock of the degree of responsiveness that is required to satisfactorily serve all constituents profitably. Responsiveness as a measure should use the concepts of floor-and-surge; lead time agility; and customer service and reverse logistics flexibility. These all are useful inputs to determine the right level of responsiveness that is required to survive and thrive in a fickle, consumer-preference driven world that is always changing.

We often find that companies use the marketplace as an excuse to not offer any stability in their supply chain and are forever fighting fires. It's as unacceptable as not considering customer/consumer preferences in your business and supply chain strategy. We encourage companies to take a hard look at the required level of agility in the end-to-end supply chain and then to innovate their processes using techniques such as lean to extract an additional 3 to 5 percent year-over-year improvements (the "Rule of 5 percent"). At some point, all companies will reach a ceiling of agility and improvement. The hope is that with continued innovation and growth on the top line, it will be a very long journey.

Driving the Next Idea

As our discipline continues to gain importance as a strategic enabler for competitive advantage, we have to demonstrate innovative ideas that will continue to drive increased levels of investment. The entire supply chain management ecosystem (academics, practitioners, technology providers, consulting firms, and so on) all have distinct roles in continuing to drive the agenda forward.

To achieve that end, all of us need to become much more cross functional and "extra enterprise" focused. Cost pressures are making this a necessity and not a luxury, and the group that is able to extract value where none was expected will truly become the supply chain master. We hope that the ten ideas offered here will help supply chain organizations deliver on that value proposition- and in the process drive the next new idea.

NOTES FROM CHAPTER

UNSHACKLED PART XV

Looking into the Crystal Ball

This section has been a staple in my previous books as well. We will attempt to lay the foundation for advances that may become main stream in the next decade or so. We call it the crystal ball effect i.e. try to predict based on sound judgment and pragmatic outlook across Industries as well as factoring in existing economic conditions that will seem to continue for the foreseeable future.

Here are the top ten trends that we see impacting the field of global supply chain management over the next decade:

TREND I: MULTIPLE SUPPLY CHAINS WITHIN THE SAME CORPORATION AND BUSINESS UNIT WILL BE PAR FOR THE COURSE

The days when a single Design to Delivery process worked across all products, channels and geographies has disappeared for ever. Companies will have to deal with different design clock speeds; fulfillment routines; manufacturing cycle times as well as continued emphasis on severe customer penalties for missed service. It is impossible to create a single supply chain that will be able to deal with all the variations of the above processes. Hence, what we will have to design is a segmentation of supply chains based on common denominators of the design to delivery process and align our assets and human resources across the multiple denominators. We see that in the suture companies will need to have an initial product entry supply chain; a replenishment driven supply chain and finally a product sun setting supply chain.

TREND II: RULE OF 5% IS A MANDATORY KPI

The rule of 5% is one in which every supply chain process will be required to provide a 5% improvement YOY based on the key performance indicators (KPI's) for that function. Maintaining status quo will be unacceptable; however 5% improvement does not necessarily translate to a cost reduction but can be in the form of efficiency gain; human productivity gains as well as adoption of technology to further automation.

Trend III: Supply chains will become Service chains

The product will essentially become a table stake for all companies. The power of brands has been diminishing over the years as consumers and customers continue to become value driven (essentially we are talking about the 80% of products that can be viewed as commodities and not the 20% luxury items that will continue to remain). The branded companies have been propping up declining Gross margins by allowing for promotion and coop discounts. They have eroded their Net margins significantly over the years. We see that the service component to every product will become the future and companies will have to engineer their supply chains to deliver services such as product knowledge; in store merchants; information kiosks; customer and consumer chat portals; as well as figure out ways to get higher consumer and customer touch points post the product sale. Supply Chains will become similar to the old razor and blade routine where you give away the razor at a reasonable / low price to lock in the consumer for the blades. The supply chain will become the razor and the service chain will become the blades.

Trend IV: Supply Chains will need to be shortened by an average of 30%

Supply chain design to delivery times will need to continue to shorten over the next decade. We estimate that across industries an average reduction in cycle time will be about 20 – 30% in order to satisfy increasing consumer and customer needs; continued pressure on top line growth as well as increasing global consumption.

Trend V: Information Technology adoption for supply chain management will become SAS (software as a service) centric

The days of large monolithic investments in information technology projects are dead. The future is going to be filled with agility and shorter pay as you go type of investments. Most companies will adopt "cloud based" technology offerings to augment their existing investments. They will continue to invest in value added decision support technology and intelligent analytics to further drive efficiencies and improvements across all aspects of the supply chain.

Trend VI: Planning of supply chains will be replaced by the ability to rapidly replan

Supply chains will need to become very agile and rethink the way that plans are laid out and executed. The emphasis in the future will be on the company's ability to execute and re plan as opposed to continue in the quest for the perfect initial plan. Planning will become more localized in its optimality and the quest for the global and static optimal solution will inherently take a back seat.

Trend VII: Companies will outsource all non-core supply chain processes and functions

Supply Chain process outsourcing and out tasking will become mainstream across all functions such as planning; scheduling; customer and consumer service; fulfillment and logistics; etc. We offer the conjecture that in the future supply chain process functions will follow the same trend as Information Services and will be largely outsourced.

Trend VIII: On tap services that will be delivered globally will become main stream

Following in the footsteps of the prior trend, services that will be delivered to satisfy supply chain process requirements will also be available "on tap" or as needed. These skills and services will be delivered globally and will be charged for in similar fashion to the "software as a service" model.

Trend IX: Global skill development will become necessary to satisfy the demands for supply chain professionals

We are not producing enough qualified candidates to satisfy increasing demands. Additionally, a large portion of our demand will continue to be for positions outside of the US. This will require us to tap into and help develop global skill bases. Efforts are already underway with collaborative efforts within universities globally. We believe that companies will need to alter their recruiting and retention mechanisms to focus on the global talent pool and not restrict themselves to a local talent pool. Additionally, executives in the US will need to provide guidance and coaching to universities and institutions in places such as China, India, Singapore and Philippines to tap into the huge talent pool that is available in those geographies.

Trend X: Chief Supply Chain Officer's positions will continue in their rise into the boardroom and will become akin to the Chief of Staff role in many countries

Supply Chain Management has continued it's meteoric rise in stature over the last decade where it is definitely a board room topic. However, it is still not a consistent board room seat. This will change rapidly in the next decade and the position will become one of the most important if not the most important position in any company (next to the CEO). The position and its associated span and impact on the company's profitability will make it a position that is very similar to the Chief of Staff role in many countries.

NOTES FROM CHAPTER

APPENDIX

Figures from Unshackled Part I

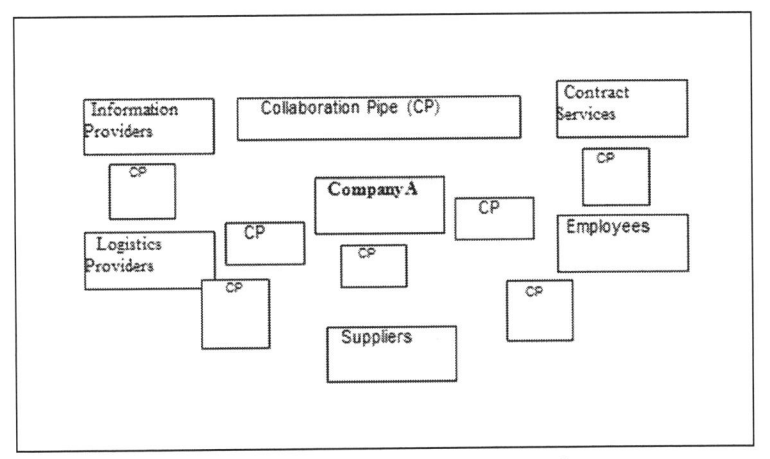

Figure One: The value community

Area	Traditional	Value Community	Extended Value Community
Focus	Internal	Varies depending on function	External or Market facing
Leverage	Minimal	Some	Optimal
Competitive Nature	Not competitive	Competitive	Extremely Competitive but still focused on the brand
Information Management	Silos and disparate	Some sharing but mainly disparate	Common platform or data streams for strategic functions
Strength of Partnerships	Not strong	Strong based on functions	Strong in all functions and retains only core
Participation in Networked Economy	Minimal	Some	Key anchor for ecosystem

Figure Two: The Traditional to Extended spectrum

Figures from Unshackled Part II

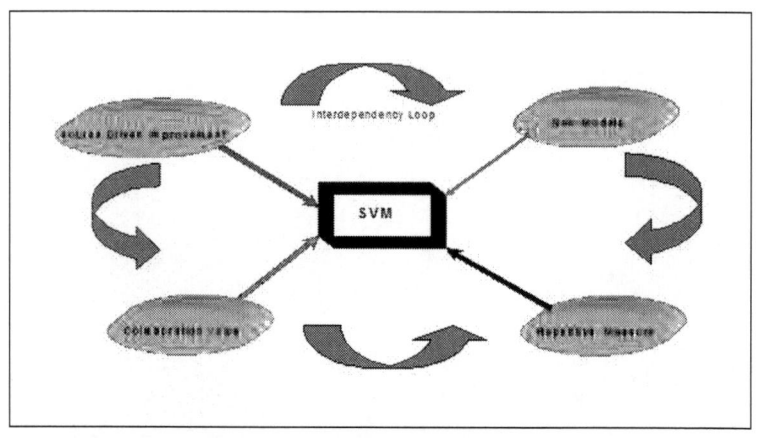

Figure 1: An SVM Framework

Working Capital	Inventory turns	H	H	H	M
Fixed Capital	Asset leverage	L	H	H	M
Service Level	As measured by key customers	H	H	H	M
Strength of partnerships	Degree of virtuality and dis-intermediation	L	H	H	M
Market Penetration	Number of new channels, geographies and product innovation	L	M	L	H
Revenue Lift	In stock percentage at end consumption point	L	M	H	H
Ecosystem Alignment	Metrics of participants that are in common	L	L	M	H

Figure 2: Sample computational metrics

APPENDIX

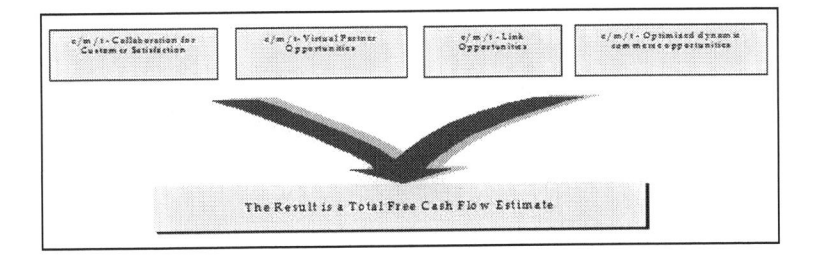

Figure 3: Sample SVM calculation

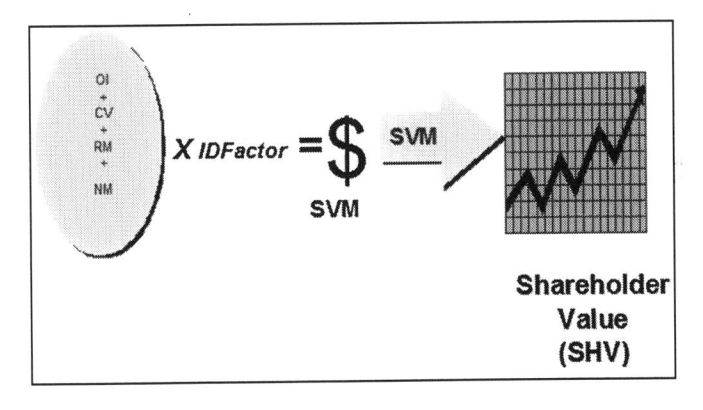

Figure 4: Convert EVC Impact to Shareholder Value

Figures from Unshackled Part III

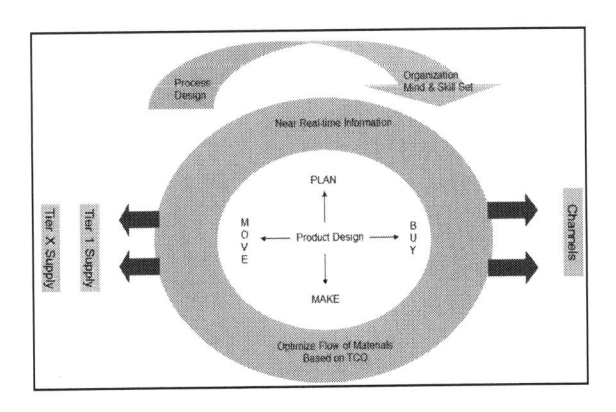

Exhibit 1: The Delivery to Delivery Framework

SUPPLY CHAINS UNSHACKLED

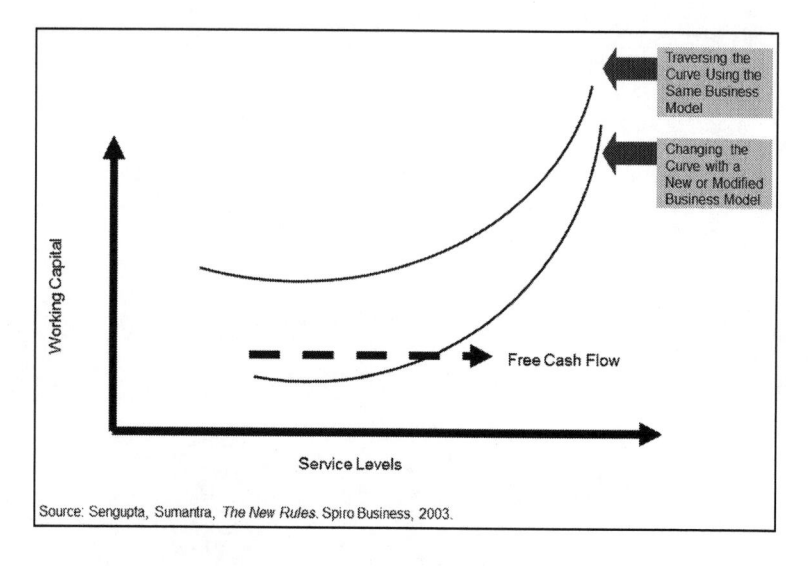

Source: Sengupta, Sumantra, *The New Rules*. Spiro Business, 2003.

Exhibit 2: Moving the Business Curve

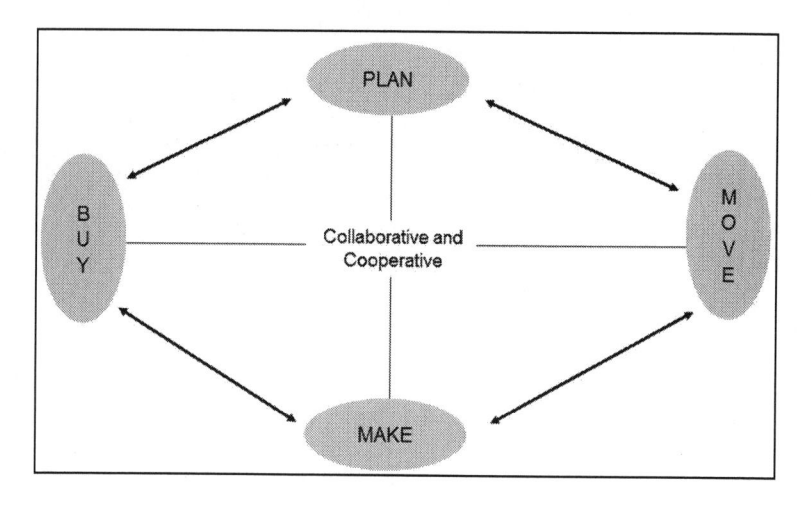

Exhibit 3: The Leveraged Value Chain

APPENDIX

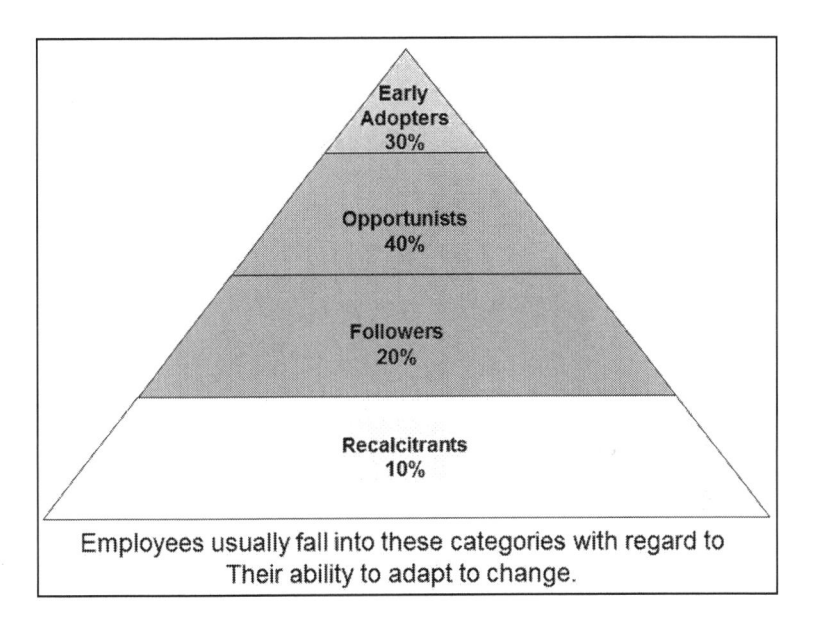

```
                    Early
                  Adopters
                    30%

                 Opportunists
                    40%

                  Followers
                    20%

                 Recalcitrants
                    10%
```

Employees usually fall into these categories with regard to
Their ability to adapt to change.

Exhibit 4: The Human Adaptation Pyramid

Figures from Unshackled Part IV

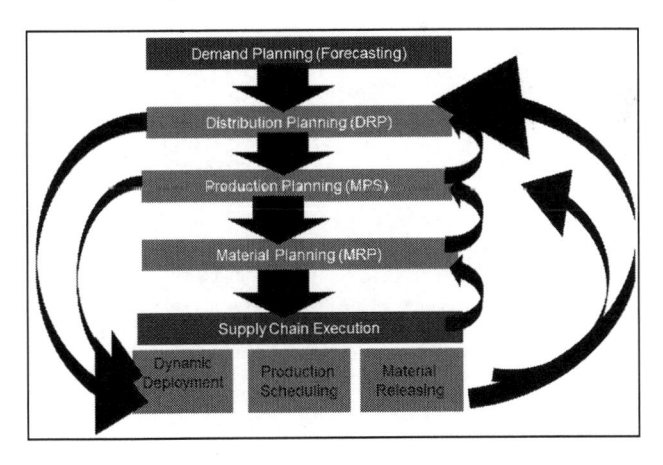

Demand Planning (Forecasting)
Distribution Planning (DRP)
Production Planning (MPS)
Material Planning (MRP)
Supply Chain Execution
Dynamic Deployment | Production Scheduling | Material Releasing

Exhibit 1: The Traditional Planning Process

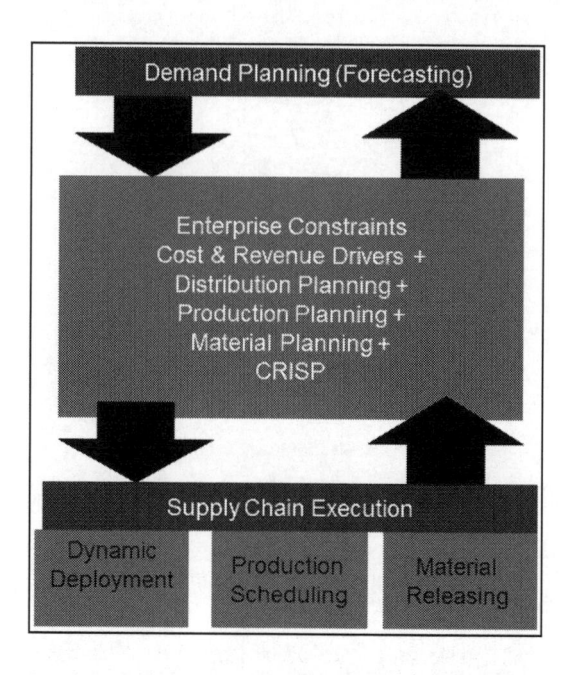

Exhibit 2: Planning Process Flow Using CRISP

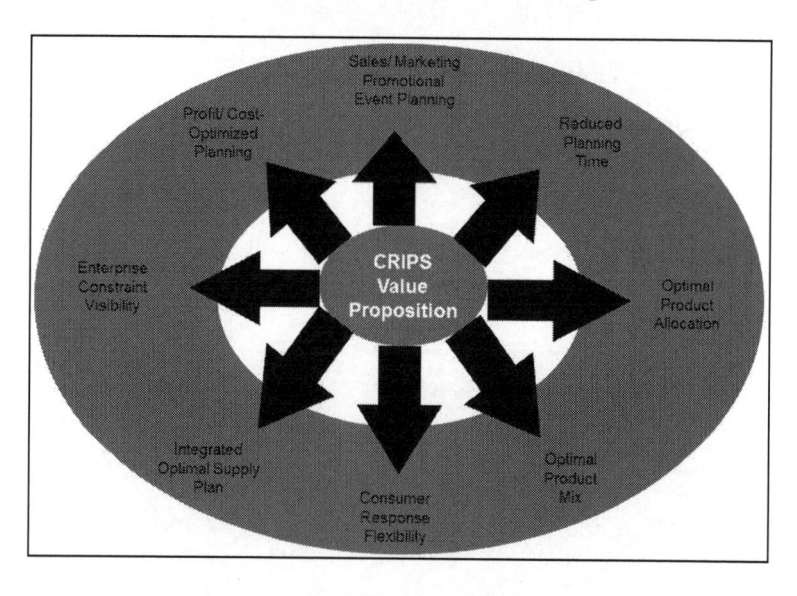

Exhibit 3: Value Proposition for CRISP

APPENDIX

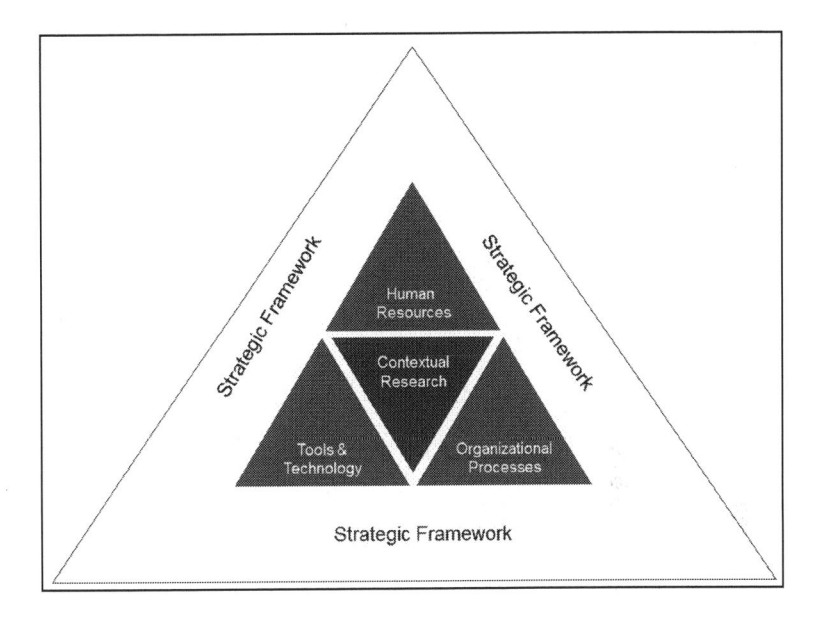

Exhibit 4: Core Components of CRISP Implementation

Figures from Unshackled Part V

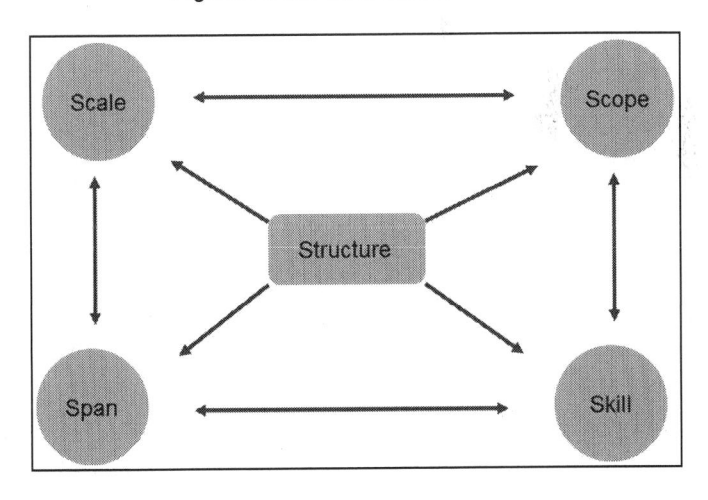

Exhibit 1: The "5s" Model

249

S number	Dimensions needed to define and execute
Scope – 1st	Process and P&L for Channel
Span – 2nd	Physical and Functional
Scale – 3rd	Virtual vs. Vertical; Type of virtuality and degree of virtuality
Skill – 4th	Mix and Type
Structure – 5th	Physical; Functional and Informational

Exhibit 2: Table Key Aspects of Each "S"

Figures from Unshackled Part VI

Options		Physical	Information	Process
	Separate and Operate	H	H	H
	Share and Operate	M/H	M/H	M/H
	Joint Operation	L/M	L/M	L/M

Degree of Separation: H= High, M= Moderate, L=Low

Exhibit 1: Degrees of Separation

APPENDIX

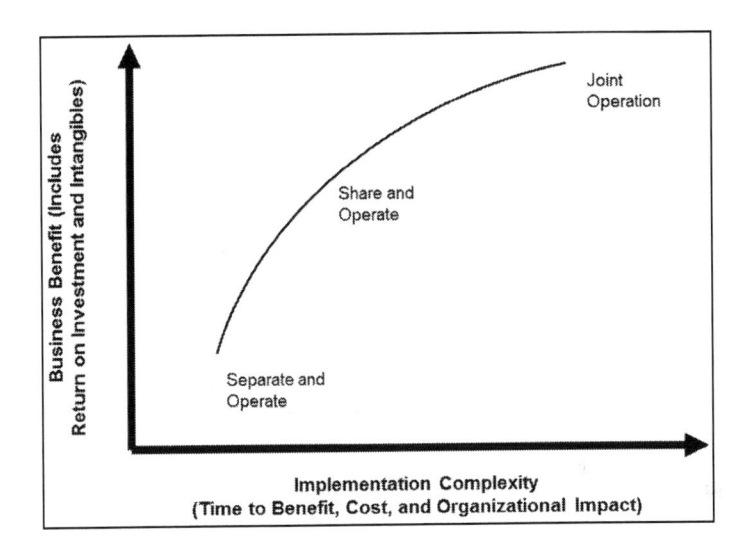

Exhibit 2: Business Benefit vs. Implementation Complexity

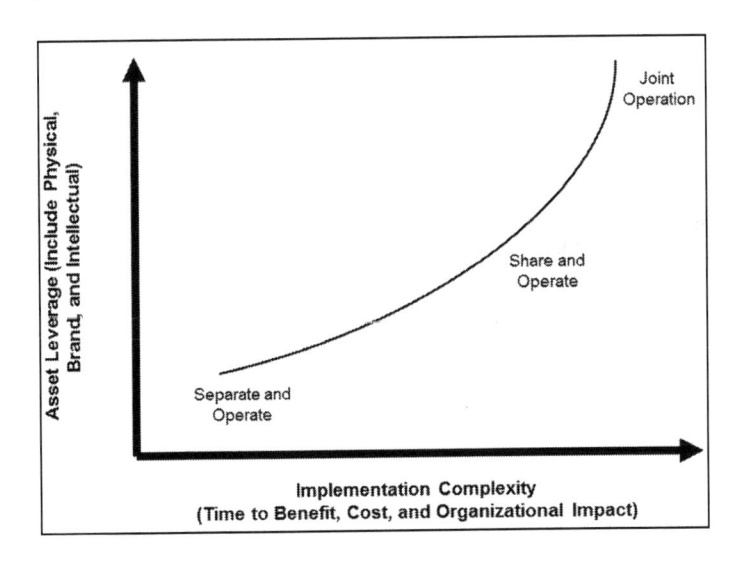

Exhibit 3: Asset Leverage vs. Implementation Complexity

Figures from Unshackled Part VII

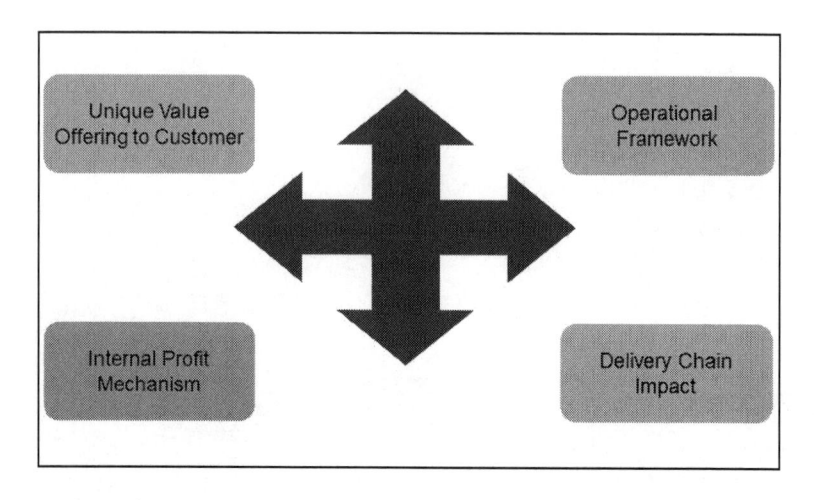

Exhibit 1: Four Components of the B2B Framework

Marketplace's Ability to Sustain Revenue Stream Over Life Cycle	Initiate	Penetrate	Mainstream
Commerce	M	L	L
Connectivity	L	M	M/H
Collaboration	L	M	H
Content	L	L	M
Community	L	M	M

L= Low, M= Medium, H= High

Exhibit 2: Marketplace's Ability to Sustain Revenue

APPENDIX

Types of Revenue	Transaction-based	Membership/Subscription Based	Combination
Commerce		———	
Connectivity		———	
Collaboration			———
Content		———	
Community		———	

Exhibit 3: Type of Revenue, Transaction, Membership, Combo

Figures from Unshackled Part IX

It's The People ...

Projects will encounter problems of all kinds, but the most severe issues tend to be human resource- and people-related.

TYPE OF ISSUE	LOW	MEDIUM	HIGH
People-related only		X	X
Process-related only	X		
Process- and technology-related		X	X
People-, process-, and technology-related		X	X
People- and technology-related			X
People- and process-related			X
Technology-related only	X	X	
Measurement- and incentive-related			X

Figure One: Issues Matrix

253

SUPPLY CHAINS UNSHACKLED

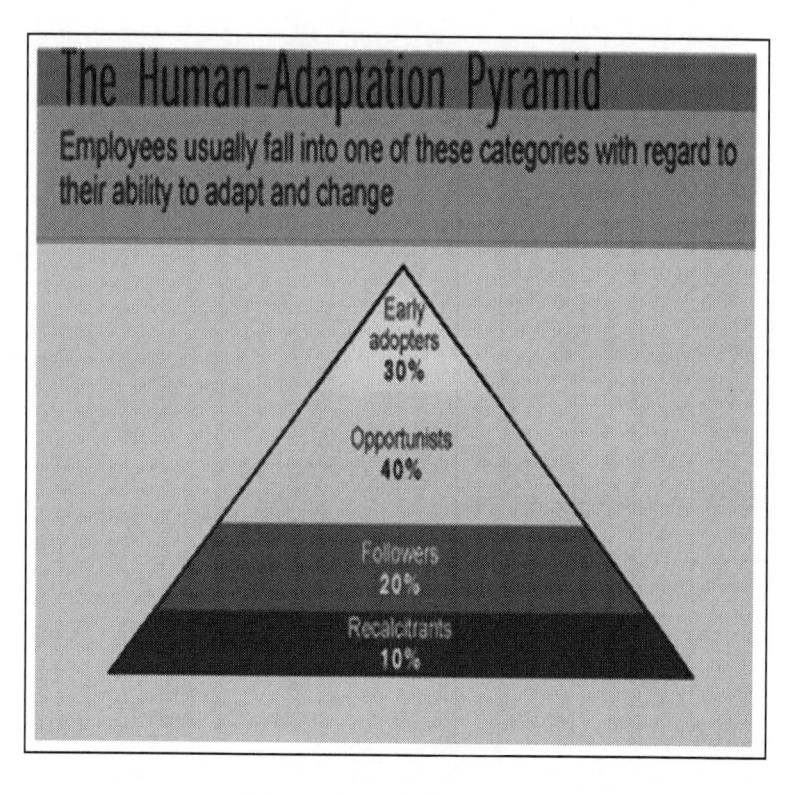

The Human-Adaptation Pyramid
Employees usually fall into one of these categories with regard to their ability to adapt and change

- Early adopters 30%
- Opportunists 40%
- Followers 20%
- Recalcitrants 10%

Figure Two: The Pyramid

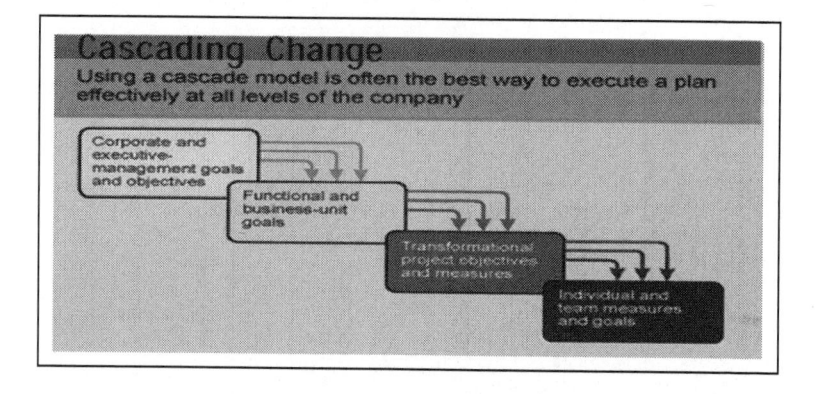

Cascading Change
Using a cascade model is often the best way to execute a plan effectively at all levels of the company

- Corporate and executive-management goals and objectives
- Functional and business-unit goals
- Transformational project objectives and measures
- Individual and team measures and goals

Figure Three: The cascade

254

APPENDIX

Figures from Unshackled Part X

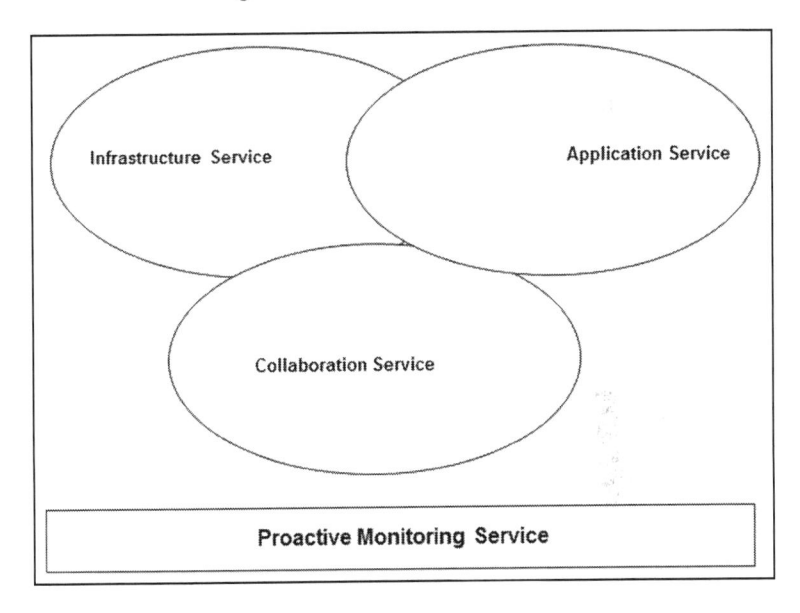

Figure One: EVC Information Management Model

Function \ Responsibility	CIO	CTO
Technology Strategy	S / P	P / S
Application Strategy	S / P	P / S
Evolving Needs for People and Process	S / P	P / S
Major project implementation	P / S	S / P
Role in promoting EVC	Inward focus	Outward Focus
Day to Day operation	P / S	S / P

Figure Two: Primary vs. Secondary Responsibility

255

SUPPLY CHAINS UNSHACKLED

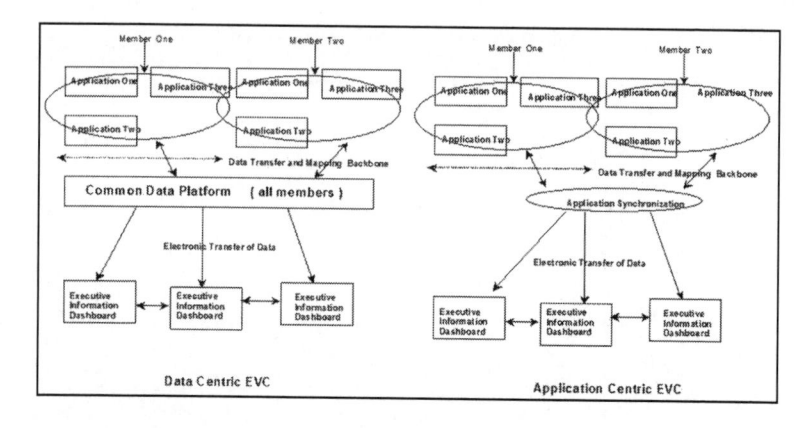

Figure Three: Data Centric View vs. Application Centric View

Characteristics \ Approach	Data Centric	Application Centric
Ease of maintaining data integrity	Relatively easy	Difficult
Business Need driven	May be IT driven at times	Majority
Modular extensions	Relatively Easy	Can be difficult
Scalable to VC	Relatively easy	Can be difficult if on different platforms
Scalable to EVC	Relatively easy	Can be difficult if on different platforms
Degree of standardization	High	Ad Hoc
Ability to perform Peer to Peer transactions	Easy through CDP	Can be difficult if on different platforms
Executive Information sharing	Relatively Easy	Difficult if on different platforms

Figure Four: Ease of use in DC and AC

APPENDIX

Function : Category and Time Frame	Category	0 – 3 months	4 – 8 months	9 + months
1. EEB	B	X	X	
2. IT Integration	S		X	
3. Supplier, Customer and Key relationship enablement	S/R		X	X
4. Collaborative Business Planning	S/R		X	X
5. Collaborative Design	R			X
6. Collaborative Logistics	S/R		X	X
7. Collaborative Working Capital Streamlining	B/S/R	X	X	X
8. Collaborative Trade	R			X
9. Electronic Cash to Cash	S/R		X	X
10. Executive Monitoring	R			X
11. Scalable Infrastructure	R			X
12. Global Representation	S/R			X
13. Emerging Decision Analytic tools	R			X
14. Community Content Management	S/R		X	X
15. Customer Service	S		X	
16. Customer Management	R			X
17. Community Data Repository	S/R		X	X
18. Community Process Excellence Team	R			X
19. Community Technical Excellence Team	R			X
20. Community Data Integrity Function	R			X
21. Community Information Usage team	R			X

Figure Five: The Information Management Framework

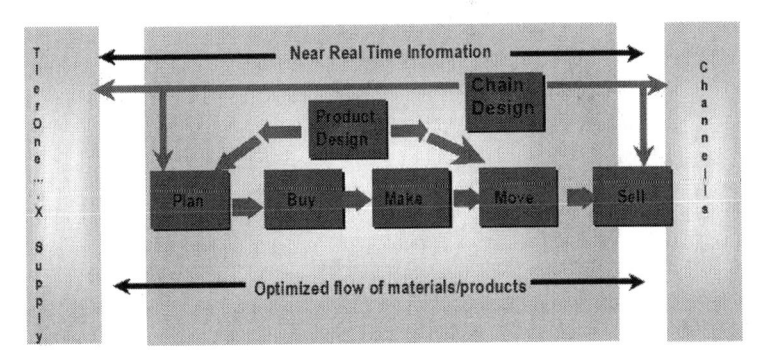

Figures from Unshackled Part XI

Figure One: Traditional Supply Chain Flow

257

SUPPLY CHAINS UNSHACKLED

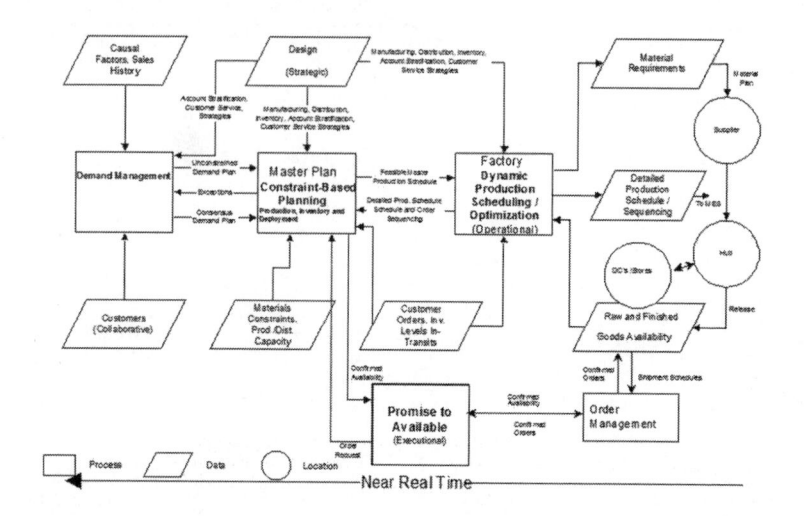

Figure Two: Information Flow in a traditional Supply Chain

Type of Information	Strategic	Collaborative	Operational / Tactical
Capacity		X	X
Capability	X	X	
Pricing	X		
Point Of Sale or Consumption	X	X	
Participants	X	X	
Locations	X		
Bill Of Material			X
Forecast		X	
Schedule			X
Constraints		X	X
Inventory	X	X	
Lead Times		X	X
Calendar			X

Figure Three: Classifying Data Types

APPENDIX

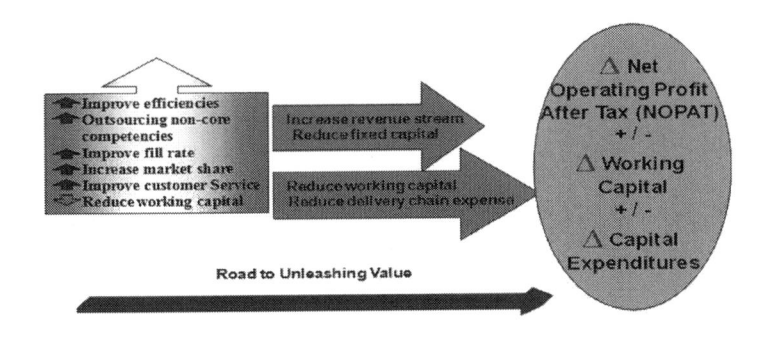

Figure Four: Value Levers for SCM

Process Areas	Type of Virtuality / Arrangement
Purchasing	Centralized or GPO
Logistics	Outsourced completely or shared service
Planning	ASP model
Manufacturing	Contract
Sales and Service	Distributors or Shared model for end customer interaction

Figure Five: Types of Outsourced Arrangements

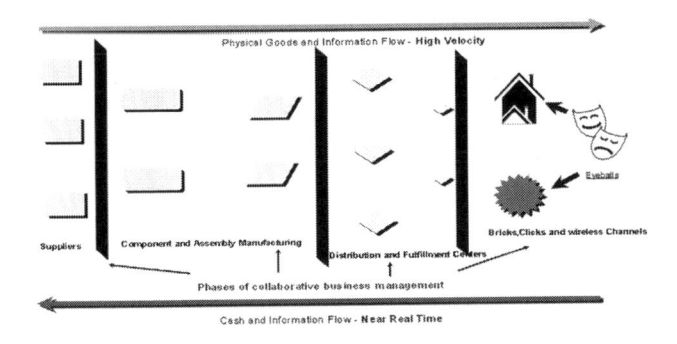

Figure Six – Networked Collaboration

SUPPLY CHAINS UNSHACKLED

Figures from Unshackled Part XII

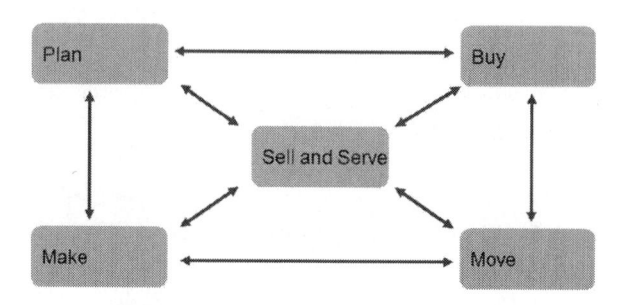

Exhibit 1: Mega Supply Chain Process

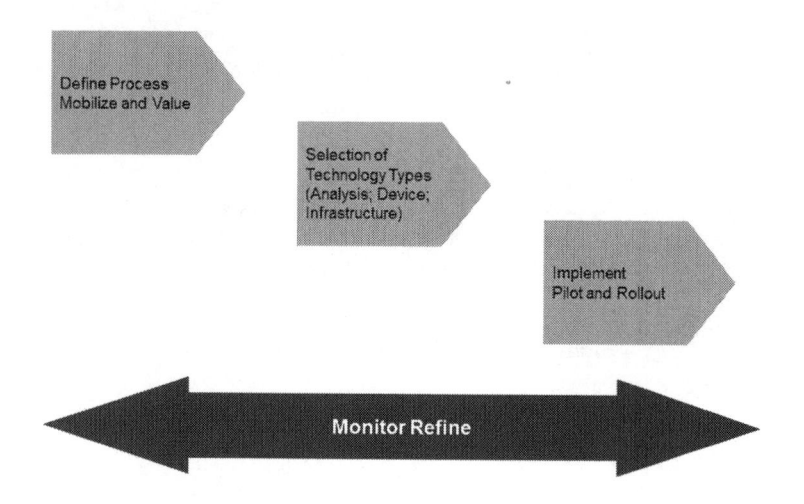

- Plan
- Buy
- Sell and Serve
- Make
- Move

Exhibit 2: Mobility Implementation Approach

- Define Process Mobilize and Value
- Selection of Technology Types (Analysis; Device; Infrastructure)
- Implement Pilot and Rollout
- Monitor Refine

APPENDIX

Figures from Unshackled Part XIII

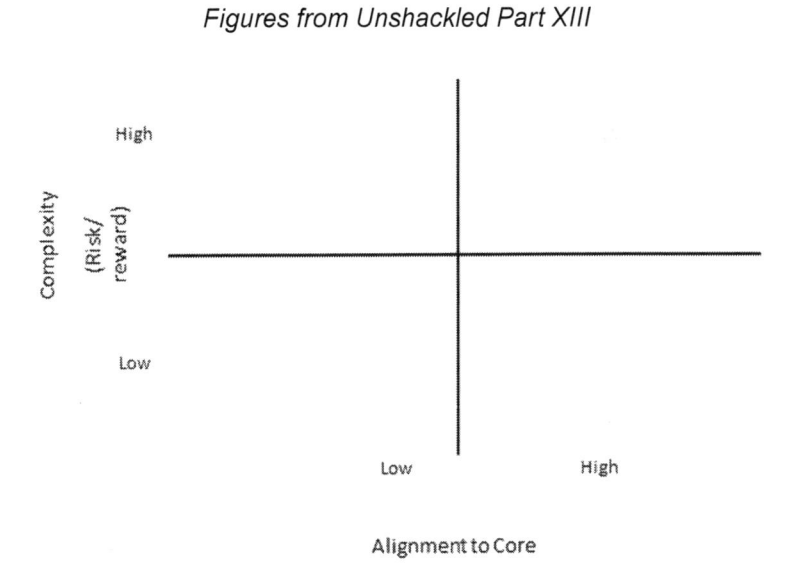

Complexity (Risk/reward) — vertical axis: High / Low
Alignment to Core — horizontal axis: Low / High

Figure One: Complexity Tradeoffs

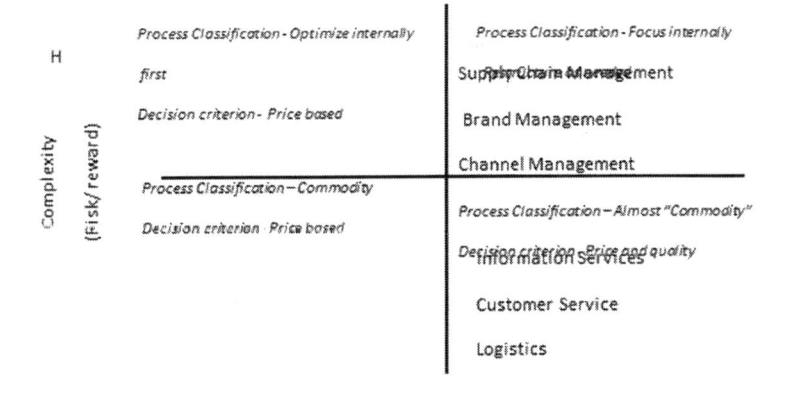

H	*Process Classification - Optimize internally first*	*Process Classification - Focus internally*
		Supply Chain Management
	Decision criterion - Price based	Brand Management
Complexity (Risk/reward)		Channel Management
	Process Classification – Commodity	*Process Classification – Almost "Commodity"*
	Decision criterion - Price based	*Decision criterion - Price and quality*
		Information Services
		Customer Service
		Logistics

Figure Two: Process and Operating criterion matrix

261

SUPPLY CHAINS UNSHACKLED

Factor	Weight (between 0 and 1 and adds to 1)	Importance (H = 3; M = 2; L=1)
Delivery model of the service i.e. on site vs. self service vs. off site		
Quality of current service vs. desired quality		
Price of current service vs. future (include upgrades and quality)		
Flexibility desired (time spent vs. focus vs. cost)		
Industry knowledge required to perform service		
Openness of company to inter and intra company problem resolutions		

Figure Three: A Sample Scorecard

Figures from Unshackled Part XIV

The Design-to- Delivery Framework

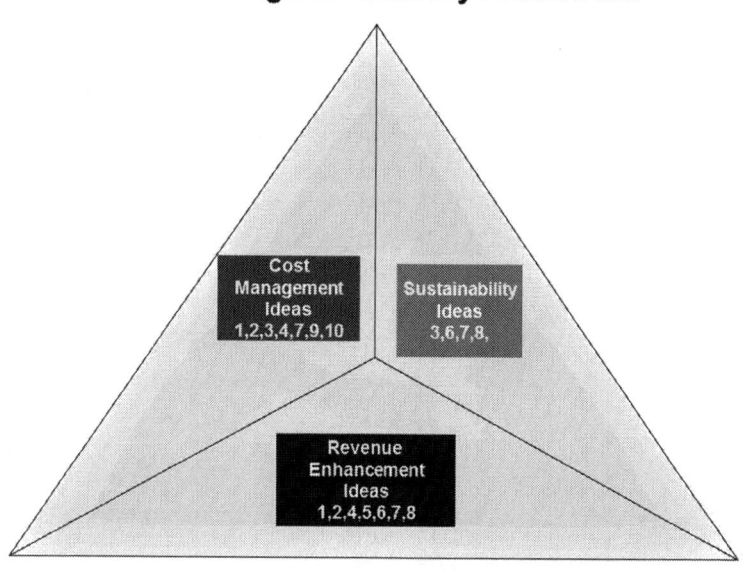

Cost Management Ideas
1,2,3,4,7,9,10

Sustainability Ideas
3,6,7,8,

Revenue Enhancement Ideas
1,2,4,5,6,7,8

262

Made in the USA
Columbia, SC
20 July 2023